Landmarks of world literature

Gabriel García Márquez

ONE HUNDRED YEARS OF SOLITUDE

Landmarks of world literature

General Editor: J. P. Stern

GABRIEL GARCÍA MÁRQUEZ

One Hundred Years
of Solitude

MICHAEL WOOD
University of Exeter

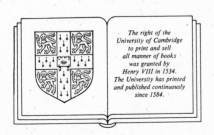

The right of the
University of Cambridge
to print and sell
all manner of books
was granted by
Henry VIII in 1534.
The University has printed
and published continuously
since 1584.

CAMBRIDGE UNIVERSITY PRESS

Cambridge
New York   Port Chester
Melbourne   Sydney

Published by the Press Syndicate of the University of Cambridge
The Pitt Building, Trumpington Street, Cambridge CB2 1RP
40 West 20th Street, New York, NY 10011, USA
10 Stamford Road, Oakleigh, Melbourne 3166, Australia

© Cambridge University Press 1990

First published 1990

Printed in Great Britain at the University Press, Cambridge

British Library cataloguing in publication data
Wood, Michael
Gabriel García Márquez: One hundred years of
solitude − (Landmarks of world literature)
1. Fiction in Spanish. Colombian writers. García
Márquez, Gabriel. Critical studies
I. Title   II. Series
863

Library of Congress cataloguing in publication data
Wood, Michael, 1936–
Gabriel Garcia Márquez: One hundred years of solitude / Michael
Wood.
     p.   cm. − (Landmarks of world literature)
Includes bibliographical references.
ISBN 0–521–32823–3. − ISBN 0–521–31692–8 (pbk.)
1. García Márquez, Gabriel, 1928–   − Criticism and
interpretation.   2. García Márquez, Gabriel. 1928− Cien años de
soledad.   I. Title.   II. Series.
PQ8180.17.A73Z96   1990
863–dc20   89–22332   CIP

ISBN 0 521 32823 3 hard covers
ISBN 0 521 31692 8 paperback

Contents

vi   Contents

Chronology

	García Márquez's life and works	*Related historical and literary events*
1899		United Fruit Company arrives in Colombia.
1899–1902		Colombian civil wars of half a century culminate in the War of the Thousand Days. The Treaty of Neerlandia is signed. The only difference between the warring Liberals and Conservatives, Colonel Aureliano Buendía says at the end of his military and political career, is that the Liberals go to mass at 5 and the Conservatives go to mass at 8.
1909–35		Juan Vicente Gómez is dictator of Venezuela.
1919		Colombia signs contract with Tropical Oil Company.
1922, 1935		Colombia's border disputes with Venezuela and Peru settled.
1924		José Eustacio Rivera, *La Vorágine (The Vortex)*.
1928	Gabriel José García Márquez born 6 March, in Aracataca, in tropical northern Colombia. This is the date usually given, and 6 March is certainly right. The author's father says the child was born a year earlier, and so reportedly do those who have seen the birth certificate.	Major strike of banana workers near Santa Marta, in northern Colombia, ending in a massacre.
1928–36	Lives in Aracataca in the house of his maternal grandfather, Colonel Nicolás Ricardo Márquez Mejía, surrounded by aunts and memories and the rumour of ghosts. Later in life he dreams repeatedly that he has never left this house. He says, 'Nothing has happened to me since'. An early draft of *One Hundred Years of Solitude* was called *The House*.	

1929		Rómulo Gallegos, *Doña Bárbara*.
1936–9		Civil War in Spain.
1936–46	Primary and secondary school in Barranquilla and then Zipaquira, in the highlands of Colombia. At age 13 he sees the capital, Bogotá, for the first time, 'a distant, gloomy city where an unrelenting drizzle had been falling since the beginning of the sixteenth century . . . interminable funerals . . . and corpses from important families who thought they had invented death'.	
1941		United Fruit Company leaves Colombia, or at least drastically reduces its presence.
1944		Jorge Luis Borges, *Ficciones*.
1947–9	Studies law at the National University, Bogotá, and at the University of Cartagena. Publishes first stories in the Saturday supplement of a Bogotá newspaper, *El Espectador*. Writes a column for *El Universal*, of Cartagena.	
1948–57		Profuse and continued violence in Colombia, generically known as La Violencia, following the assassination of the Liberal leader Jorge Gaitán. Different assessments put the number of people killed in these quarrels at 200,000 or more than 300,000.
1949		Alejo Carpentier, *El reino de este mundo* (*The Kingdom of this World*).

1950		William Faulkner receives Nobel Prize.
1950–5	Gives up law studies and becomes a full-time journalist, working for *El Heraldo* and *El Nacional*, both Barranquilla papers, and for *El Espectador*. Publishes more stories, and a first novel, *Leaf Storm*, 1955.	
1953		General Gustavo Rojas Pinilla seizes power in Colombia.
1954–8		Pérez Jiménez is dictator of Venezuela.
1955		Juan Rulfo, *Pedro Páramo*.
1955–7	In Europe as correspondent of *El Espectador*. Takes a film-making course in Rome. Rojas Pinilla closes *El Espectador*, and the jobless and moneyless García Márquez stays in Paris, finishing and reworking *No one writes to the Colonel*, published 1961. He visits several socialist countries and writes *90 Days Behind the Iron Curtain*.	
1957		Rojas Pinilla resigns. A military junta announces elections, which are held in 1958. Coalition governments follow, but there is much unrest and guerilla activity.
1958	Marries Mercedes Barcha in Barranquilla, works in Caracas for the magazines *Momento*, *Elite* and *Venezuela gráfica*. Writes most of the stories to be published in *Big Mama's Funeral*, 1962.	
1959		Alejo Carpentier, *Los pasos perdidos* (*The Lost Steps*). Fidel Castro's forces take Havana; President Batista resigns and flees.

1959–61	In Havana to report on the trials known as Operación Verdad. Starts office of Cuban press agency *Prensa Latina* in Bogotá; works for *Prensa Latina* in Havana and New York.	
1961		Juan Carlos Onetti, *El astillero (The Shipyard)*. Failed anti-Castrist invasion at the Bay of Pigs.
1961–7	Mexico City. Edits magazines *Sucesos* and *La Familia*. Works for an advertising agency and wins a Colombian prize for his novel *In Evil Hour*, 1962. Works on several film scripts. Writes and publishes *One Hundred Years of Solitude*, 1967. Instant, overwhelming success. The book is translated into 27 languages, wins 4 international prizes, runs through hundreds of editions. It is said to be the most popular book in Spanish since *Don Quixote*. García Márquez had started and abandoned the book when he was 17 or 18, failing to find the right tone. 'I had to live for 20 years and write 4 books of apprenticeship to discover that . . . the story had to be told, simply, the way my grandparents told it'. 'I've never been really interested,' he said later, 'in any idea which can't withstand many years of neglect'. His ideas for *The Autumn of the Patriarch* and *Chronicle of a Death Foretold* were respectively left to ripen for 17 and 30 years.	
1962		International crisis concerning the installation of Soviet missile bases in Cuba.
1963		Julio Cortázar, *Rayuela (Hopscotch)*.

1965	Mario Vargas Llosa, *La casa verde* (*The Green House*). Guillermo Cabrera Infante, *Tres tristes tigres* (*Three Sad Tigers*).
1966	José Lezama Lima, *Paradiso*.
1967	Carlos Fuentes, *Cambio de piel* (*Change of Skin*). Che Guevara dies in Bolivia.
1967–75	Barcelona. Receives an honorary degree from Columbia University, New York. Publishes *Innocent Eréndira*, 1972. Helps to found *Alternativa*, a Bogotá review dedicated to political opposition. Becomes a vice-president of the Russell Tribunal. Publishes *The Autumn of the Patriarch*, 1975.
1970	José Donoso, *El obsceno pájaro de noche* (*The Obscene Bird of Night*). Salvador Allende elected president of Chile.
1973	Allende overthrown.
1974	Augusto Roa Bastos, *Yo el supremo* (*The Dictator*).
1975	Franco dies.
1975–81	Mexico City and Bogotá. Works on several film scripts; visits and writes on Angola and Nicaragua. Energetic political activity. He is a founder member of the Colombian party *Firmes*; works on a UNESCO report on communications; forms HABEAS, an organization for the help of political prisoners. Publishes *Chronicle of a Death Foretold*, 1981.
1979	The Somoza family, in power in Nicaragua since 1937, is ousted by the Sandinistas.

1981   Mario Vargas Llosa, *La guerra del fin del mundo* (*The War of the End of the World*).
President Omar Torrijos of Panama dies in a plane crash.

1982   Nobel Prize.
1983–   Lives in Colombia and Mexico. Publishes *Love in the Time of Cholera*, 1985.
Continues political activity.
Publishes *The General in his Labyrinth*, 1989.

A note on translation and quotations

I have used Gregory Rabassa's familiar and effective translation of *One Hundred Years of Solitude* whenever I could, which was most of the time. Where it wasn't accurate or didn't reflect the point I was after in the Spanish, I have either adapted it or offered my own wording entirely. Quotations are identified on the page, Spanish text first, e.g. [216:231]. References are to the readily available editions by Editorial Sudamericana, 1967 and Avon, 1971.

Chapter 1

Contexts

We wish to learn from our critics, but it is hard for us even
to recover from them.   Randall Jarrell

The Boom

Latin American literature existed before the conquest of the
continent, although it wasn't Latin and didn't call itself
American. But it has a way of repeatedly seeming very recent, just discovered, and not only to outsiders. There are all
kinds of gaps in its history, patches of darkness or stasis, and
the Chilean José Donoso has suggested that the so-called
Boom in contemporary Latin American fiction, the surge of
vivid and challenging new writing which appeared some twenty years ago, was the product of authors who had grand-
fathers but no fathers. The literary tradition failed to offer an
immediate example, a preferred path; but this failure, once
absorbed, became a spectacular opportunity.

The Boom is identified by the English word in Spanish,
which lends a slightly exotic flavour to the enterprise, and the
hint of a drumroll: *El 'Boom'*. The phenomenon has been
much quarrelled about: seen as an invention of the media, the
phantom child of French and American publishers; as the
outlet of a literary mafia, a conspiracy of pals promoting each
others' work; as the mark of a dazzling renaissance, or even
just a naissance, the first arrival of this literature at independent life. The term itself has been found vulgar and in-
appropriate, an insult to art; yet it seems to me perfect if we
don't take it too seriously. It evokes the clumsy excitement of
the discovery of new writers, and it usefully implies that these
writers had struck oil and got rich in the territory of the

1

imagination. *One Hundred Years of Solitude* is the chief and most enduring landmark in this Boom country.

The names most frequently associated with the Boom are those of Julio Cortázar, Carlos Fuentes, Guillermo Cabrera Infante, Gabriel García Márquez and Mario Vargos Llosa, although plenty of other writers drop in and out of the company. The nationalities behind those names already tell an interesting story: an Argentinian, a Mexican, a Cuban, a Colombian, a Peruvian. There have been pan-continental literary movements before, but not many, and there is a clear sense of new allegiances here: not to individual countries but to Latin America, to the Spanish language, to modern literature, to certain views of the relation between fiction and the world. If we add that these fatherless figures had some distinguished and much-read foreign uncles – Joyce, Kafka, Hemingway, Faulkner – and that they seem to have spent their lives at the movies, an image begins to form. We need to think too of impressive native uncles like Borges and Carpentier and Onetti, although it would take a whole theory of.literary history to say why they are uncles, not fathers; why they suggest chances but don't make a lineage.

The Boom was not big enough to be a renaissance, and wasn't a movement, if by a movement we mean a school with a concerted programme. But it was an occasion of some importance in Latin America, not a cultural confection or a freakish accident. It was an assertion of self-confident modernity, it put an end to provincialism and apologies, and it can quite properly be called a movement in another definition, since it reflected the meeting of particular forces at a particular time. The time was the 1960s – perhaps the last novel which really belongs to the Boom is Donoso's *Obscene Bird of Night*, 1970 – and the forces were chiefly literary impatience and political despair.

The impatience is clear. Foreign influences on these writers, the fantastic and sentimental ingredients of loved movies, the eerie and haunting provocations of Borges, Carpentier and Onetti all helped to provide a fund of story-telling techniques just waiting to be tried out; invited a mingling of irony

and affection; conjured up a deep suspicion of professed
realism, both in and out of fiction. Carpentier spoke of the
marvels of Latin American reality, 'lo real maravilloso',
which a dutiful realism necessarily misses, and the critical cat-
chphrase *magical realism*, although full of muddle, does suggest a significant shift in literary perspective. There are considerable philosophical and historical complications here, and
perhaps it will be sufficient for the moment to say that the
writers of the Boom discovered, as if for the first time and all
at once, that the world is a fabrication and full of delirious
improbabilities but, alas, still real enough; that the imagination is nearly always right, either because someone has
already done what you have only imagined or because you
have imagined a fitting metaphor for someone's need; and
that fiction in these circumstances is both a playground and
a battlefield, *the* place where a culture's central quarrels may
be fought out and seen to be fought out.

In one sense this rich and rather nervous impatience is quite
old. Skipping the gaps, going back even beyond the grand-
fathers, we can put together an intermittent Spanish
American tradition — only retrospectively, it is true, but how
else do we usually put traditions together? The baroque, for
example, persisted in Latin America long after it had faded
in Europe, and this curious fact points us very precisely to
certain features of the writing of the Boom.

The persistence was not mere backwardness or under-
development — it can't have been in writers of the
stature of Sor Juana and Juan Ruiz de Alarcón — but the
reflection, I want to suggest, of a particular, ongoing in-
timacy with trickery and elaboration and bewilderment. One
of Sor Juana's most famous poems begins 'Verde embeleso
de la vida humana', which Samuel Beckett translates as 'Green
enravishment of human life'. It is worth noting that *embeleso*
means fascination and charm, and may be related to the
English *embezzlement*. The poem ends with a grotesque and
witty scheme for the avoidance of such green deceptions. The
poet will take her two eyes into both hands, she says, and will
not see anything unless she can touch it: 'solamente lo que

toco veo'. The title of Ruiz de Alarcón's best-known play is *La verdad sospechosa, The Suspect Truth*, and its moral is that habitual liars make even the truth sound uncertain, when they happen to tell it. The thought is traditional enough but acquires an edge in Latin America, where exceptional quantities of supposed truth seem suspect, not the truth at all; where the truth gets lost with unusual ease. The word *fiction* echoes through this literature early and late, and the importation of realism and naturalism in the nineteenth and twentieth centuries produced much honourable work but no masterpieces. With hindsight these modes can be viewed as a radical error in Latin America, since they rested on a commitment to a solid material and historical world no one there quite believed in. 'Solamente lo que toco veo' sounds like a prescription for a novel of the school of Zola, but the anxiety of the phrase, the wit which asks us to find it extravagant, suggest the novel will never be written. The Boom was the blossoming of the *other novel*, which reported everything that could be seen even in hallucinations; a modernization of the baroque, displaying the brilliant trail of its deceptions but also cherishing the fragile life of facts which in other places would seem safe and stable.

We see the movement in miniature in Borges, where well-meaning imitation fails while distortion stumbles on a truth. We see too the importance of Borges for later writers. The fact that this perception now seems rather familiar, one of the Boom's commonplaces, is a measure of how far his influence went.

For many years, in books now happily forgotten, I tried to catch in writing the flavour, the essence of the outskirts of Buenos Aires; naturally I used plenty of local words . . . and I wrote those forgettable and forgotten books; then a year ago I wrote a story called 'Death and the Compass', which is a sort of nightmare, a nightmare in which elements of Buenos Aires appear deformed by the horror of the nightmare; I think of the Paseo Colón and I call it Rue de Toulon, I think of the country houses of Adrogué and I call them Triste-le-Roy; once this story was published my friends told me that finally they had found in my writing the flavour of the edges of Buenos Aires . . .

And again, more mischievously:

I think that if there was any doubt about the authenticity of the Koran, the absence of camels would prove that it was an Arab work.

Historically, Octavio Paz says, Latin America is a European invention, 'a chapter in the history of European utopias', and this must be one source of a besetting and peculiar sense of unreality: not the metaphysical or epistemological anguish of modern Europeans, not the unease of North Americans faced with a fast-changing social and physical landscape, but something like an actor's weariness with a very long run, an old and intimate disbelief in the show, the feeling that what is happening cannot be true but must be someone else's dream. The *someone else* has all kinds of shapes and vantage points, of course, and after Independence Latin Americans inhabited different dreams. But the feeling seems to have remained. 'Lo real maravilloso' includes not only extravagant flora and fauna but some very unlikely events and characters, none the less real because they look so operatic. A character in Conrad's *Nostromo* is said to 'clench her hands with exasperation at not being able to take the public affairs of the country as seriously as the incidental atrocity of methods deserved. She saw in them a comedy of naive pretences, but hardly anything genuine except her own appalled imagination.' This character is not a native of the imaginary Costaguana, but a native (of Costaguana or of any historical country in Latin America) would no doubt share her sentiment, pointing out only that the pretences are not always naive. A feeling of unreality, in other words, *is* a part of local reality, best reported by versions of the baroque. It is the rush to practise the excited and often bewildered understanding of this insight that I have called literary impatience.

The despair is harder to gauge. At one time the Boom was thought to be the literary arm of the Cuban Revolution of 1959, an idea which would be simply ludicrous if it didn't contain the displaced beginnings of an insight. The writers in question were all left-leaning, and sympathetic to the Cuban

Revolution in its early days. Some, like García Márquez and like Cortázar until his death in 1984, continued sympathetic and more than sympathetic; others measured their distance or moved right away, like Cabrera Infante, who is now a British subject and lives in London. But this is gossip and *petite histoire*, and the displaced insight concerns the inescapability of the Cuban Revolution for all Latin Americans, however they feel about it. Literature was not the Revolution's stooge, but it did not inhabit another world.

It is impossible to exaggerate the Revolution's importance, for literature and for nearly everything else; and almost impossible to assess this importance with any clarity. I want to make only one guess, which seems to me especially relevant to García Márquez and my sense of him, but may have some force in relation to other writers. I am speaking of political despair, and what the Cuban Revolution did was both to alleviate and to complicate this feeling. It altered the notion of what was possible for Latin Americans, it showed that the apparently changeless could be changed, and determination could achieve almost anything, against astonishing odds. This, I think, is what revolutions characteristically show in their first moments. But in this case the showing only applied to a tiny island, and the rest of the sub-continent remained as it was, and periodically got worse. The example was authentic but how far would it reach? Despair became a choice, then, not a doom; you could give it up, and many did. But it was waiting for you when your faith wavered, and it would often have reality, or the bulk of reality, on its side. The possible is one of the provinces of truth, Baudelaire said, but what if it is a province you never manage to occupy? A nobly refused but always hovering despair drives much of the fiction of the Boom. The literary exuberance, the bravura displays of narrative technique, celebrate a desired freedom which is moral and political as well as artistic; but a mournful wit, a frame of mind accustomed to sorrow and graceful defeat remember the present score, count the bodies, the tortures, the seemingly eternal tyrants, the sectarian squabbles, the miles and miles to go. Gramsci's aphorism, Pessimism of the intellect, optimism of the will, might be construed here as optimism of the mind and heart but pessimism of the bones, of the sheer weight of a history which seems both unreal and unanswerable.

The writers themselves would probably not agree with this assessment, would argue, I think, for a more positive notion of possibility, and I would like to believe they are right. But the authority of their imagined worlds testifies against them. The best we can say − but this is to say a lot, and to evoke the chief source of the power of their work − is that despair is given a hard time, as earlier it wasn't, except naively and wishfully. These writers neither deny nor embrace despair, they try to shake it off. Indeed I shall argue that in *One Hundred Years of Solitude* despair is dismantled, held up as a superstition, an illusion of destiny. But it is a tempting illusion, the dismantling is discreet, easily missed; and progressives have always been bothered by the book, by what has been called its pessimistic and nihilistic strain. This strain would have been there anyway, for personal and historical reasons, but the energy of the resistance to it in the book, even the wit and mischief with which it is elaborated, owe a great deal to the complication of despair which the Cuban example provided. There have been other examples since, but none so striking, and Vargas Llosa's *Real Life of Alejandro Mayta*, 1984, where a miserably failed Peruvian revolution parallels Castro's success, helps us to see how deep disillusionment has gone in Latin America − and also, by implication, of course, what an undisappointed view of revolution might still be.

Colombia

It is possible, however, to make too much of the Pan-Americanism of contemporary writers, their forgetting of national identities. Latin Americans have parallel pasts and shared hopes and bogeys but they also have local histories, with vast variations from place to place. *One Hundred Years of Solitude* is in this respect a paradigm for the writing of the

Boom. It seems to delete difference, to reach for a common Latin American experience of time and politics, climate and culture. It does achieve this effect, but by the deletion not of difference but of names. It doesn't generalize or abstract, it takes concrete Colombian realities, and removes their labels. They don't become less Colombian, they just cease to be only Colombian.

Colombian has a long tradition of democracy, but it is a democracy of the upper classes, really a contest between rival oligarchies. The Liberals and the Conservatives who dominated nineteenth-century and most of twentieth-century politics stood for quite different things – reform or reaction, free trade or protection, separation or conjunction of church and state – and the jokes about their sameness in *One Hundred Years of Solitude* are extravagances, hyperboles. But the parties did represent conflicting perspectives in what can now be seen as a rather narrow band of class interests, and they generated intense local loyalties and hatreds which were fiercely maintained even *against* people's own interests, so that they felt like Capulets and Montagues, say, rather than Democrats and Republicans. There is a shrewd and funny glance at this state of affairs in a discussion of the game of draughts/checkers in the novel. José Arcadio Buendía won't play with the priest because he can't see the point of a contest in which the adversaries are in agreement on principles. The priest, who has never thought of draughts in this light, can't bring himself to play any more [80: 86–87]. The joke is quiet and thrown away, but its range is considerable. It may suggest that José Arcadio Buendía, who is supposed to be crazy, doesn't understand draughts because he wouldn't understand war or politics or the Geneva Convention: a quixotic, challenging solitude. It may imply that much fighting in the world concerns anything but principles, which are either agreed or irrelevant – as when Colonel Aureliano Buendía discovers that both Liberals and Conservatives are battling solely for power, and are ready to trade away major points of principle in order to get it. ·

A great deal of Colombian history gets stealthily into

One Hundred Years of Solitude: the arguments over reform
in the nineteenth century, the arrival of the railway, the War
of the Thousand Days, the American fruit company, the
cinema, the automobile, the massacre of striking plantation
workers which took place in the year of García Márquez'
birth — or the year after if he was born in 1927. Lucila Inés
Mena plots these correspondences with great care, and
perhaps the chief merit of Stephen Minta's book on García
Márquez (see the Guide to further Reading for a note on both
critics) is its sense of him as a specifically Colombian writer,
a man who possesses the history his characters and many of
his compatriots desperately lack.

But the most startling fact of modern Colombian history,
a fit of violence known simply as the Violence, in the way we
refer to the Troubles in Northern Ireland, has no direct expression in *One Hundred Years of Solitude*. The violence
came from guerrillas, gangsters, self-defence groups, the
police, the army; and some 200,000 people (the low estimate)
died in it. When it was said to be over, or more or less under
control, in 1962, there were still 200 civilian deaths a month.
The Violence was inescapable for Colombians, whether they
were personally affected by it nor not, as the Cuban Revolution was for Latin Americans generally, and indeed Robert
Dix makes just this connection: 'The struggle in the Cuban
mountains prior to Fidel Castro's ascent to power on January
1 1959 pales in extent, if not in its consequences, compared
to the virtual civil war which ravaged the Columbian coun-
tryside in the years after 1948.' The Violence provoked a
flood of fiction, and García Márquez himself addresses it in
No one Writes to the Colonel and *In Evil Hour*. He addresses
it very discreetly though, and seems uncomfortable with the
brutality of history; I don't mean distressed by it, as we all
must be, but anxious not to let it bully his art. There are
several implications here. García Márquez is a glancing
writer, best at obliquities. There are almost no villains in his
work, no situations not ravelled in complexity — the simplicity of his narrative stance is a feint, like Chaplin's seeming to
be awkward or clumsy — and he has no language for horrors

beyond wit and irony. Above all his vision concentrates on the way people live with themselves and with others, and the way they picture their world; and of course even the world of the Violence has to be seen as ordinary if that is where you live. That is how you manage to live there. The horror creeps into these works in the casualness with which curfews and corpses and unappeased hatreds are mentioned: mere normality.

It seems to make sense to say that the Violence appears in *One Hundred Years of Solitude* as the massacre of striking workers, which is violent enough and could stand as a compression and anticipation of the later phenomenon, an allusion and a synecdoche. It is true that Jorge Eliécer Gaitán, whose assassination sparked off the Violence, made his political name by investigating the 1928 strike, so there is a submerged link. Lucila Inés Mena thinks the final wind in which Macondo disappears is a 'veiled metaphor' for the Violence. But really neither the wind nor the massacre are very much like the Violence. They are cruel and clear, frightening but without mystery; terminal, efficient. The Violence is erratic, politically confused, an apocalypse in tatters; it lacks definition or measure, boundary or sense. It has all the feel of an immense tangle of unmanageable feuds. And it is the meaninglessness of the Violence, I think, which haunts *One Hundred Years of Solitude*, the lesson not that history is harsh but that it can go berserk, that mere anarchy is possible, and that we should not pretend to understand it when we don't.

Of course historians have speculated interestingly on the causes of the Violence. Economic, political and other motives obviously mingle: disaffected migrants, protection rackets, corrupt or inconsistent judges, uncertainty of property rights, conversion to cash-crop farming; what Dix calls hereditary hatreds, a sense of a general failure of government and the old parties, disjointed gestures towards a radical revolution. But we look at these factors, if we are not historians, the way we look at theories of the situation in Northern Ireland, or of violence at football matches. We adopt some, find others trivial, find others relevant without quite seeing how they add up. But even altogether they don't yield an explanation, or reduce the impression of an ungraspable pathology. The violence is not inhuman, not demonic, not some plague sent from elsewhere, it is our own contorted face. But it just grimaces back at us, seemingly beyond the reach of reason.

The characters themselves in *One Hundred Years of Solitude* offer many readings of history, although they don't call them that. The readings are usually ignorant or deluded, and often trying to get rid of history entirely. But García Márquez presents no rival or superior reading. The shape of his novel is the shape of the superstitions it contains – this is why the novel can seem hopeless – and the writer displays only scepticism, patience and wit; and a refusal of hypocrisy and all pretensions to wisdom. But this is a considerable display, however quiet-seeming, and in itself a liberation, because it allows us both to know and to disbelieve the most enchanting and seemingly indispensable of myths.

García Márquez' early works

García Márquez' early fiction (collected in English in *Innocent Eréndira and other stories*, although the title piece was written later) is memorable for its flickering moments of dialogue which the narrative can't live up to. 'Don't open that door,' a woman says, 'the hallway is full of difficult dreams.' 'Madam', a doctor says to another woman, 'your child has a grave illness: he is dead.' Most of these pieces concern marginal or scarcely imaginable conditions, like the death of someone already dead, the life of a ghost watching the living, the separate existence of a self in a mirror, the conversation of a couple who meet only in dreams. One has the sense of a young writer trying to modernize Poe, interested in states of consciousness, in metaphors of dislocation and absence.

In *Leaf Storm*, 1955, García Márquez begins to elaborate the world of Macondo, the tropical, rain-eaten banana town which is the setting of *One Hundred Years of Solitude*, and which also figures in several stories in *Big Mama's Funeral*, although not always by name. García Márquez practises a modest version of the recurrence of characters and events found in Balzac and Faulkner, so that pieces of story drift from text to text and are sometimes filled out. This cross-referencing also occurs even when, as in *No one Writes to the Colonel, In Evil Hour* and *Chronicle of a Death Foretold*, the town is not Macondo but another place in the same region of the unnamed country; a town without a railway, reached by river launch. Colonel Aureliano Buendía, for example, spent a night on the balcony of the rickety hotel in this town, on his way back to Macondo during the civil wars. The colonel to whom no one writes used to live in Macondo but left when the banana fever came. This is also a *later* town than Macondo, belongs in its main narratives to recent history and to the Violence. Macondo, as we shall see, ends in a whirlwind at a time which is not specified but can't be later than the 1940s. García Márquez has said that Macondo was destroyed in the year he was born, but for this to work we should have to put the strike and the massacre much earlier than their historical moment, since years pass and children grow up after it. Of course *no* dates of this kind are given in the novel, and we shouldn't fuss too much over a chronology which has no internal markers. What matters is that Macondo, unlike the other town, is gone and has been gone for some time; is only a memory, or not even a memory; a fiction within the fiction.

Both *No one Writes to the Colonel*, 1961, and *In Evil Hour*, 1962, offer what may be seen as fables for García Márquez' approach to language and literature. The former concerns a patient, dignified survivor of the War of the Thousand Days who is waiting vainly for his long promised pension and trying to console his sick wife in their penury. Their son has been killed in the Violence, and the colonel himself still occasionally distributes clandestine leaflets. This is an austere, sharp, touching and funny story in which the courtly colonel learns to swear, is driven to a violence of words. Earlier he had been quite opposed to such improprieties, but now finds himself saying 'shit' because no other word will do, because it is the disgraceful *mot juste*:

It had taken the colonel seventy-five years – the seventy-five years of his life, minute by minute – to reach this instant. He felt pure, explicit, invincible . . .

It is a soberly comic version of Kurtz' 'The horror!' in *Heart of Darkness*. A life is judged and the judgement says everything. But the judgement is so terse and compressed that we shall only spill it if we unpack it, and perhaps we don't have to unpack it in great logical detail. The point, I take it, in both Conrad and García Márquez, is that words can say more than sentences, exclamations more than arguments, and that a word can be a victory where other victories are unavailable.

In Evil Hour sees the same town living through a political truce. The mayor is getting rich and needs peace in order to get richer. 'We're trying to build a decent town', he says, and a poor woman sharply replies, 'This was a decent town before you people came.' The mayor has a brutal past, but the town is not much better, and when the truce ends, promising a return to chaos and slaughter, the community experiences 'a feeling of collective victory in the confirmation that was in everyone's consciousness: things hadn't changed'. This feeling, this sour embrace of the worst expectation, is what the Cuban Revolution altered, at least for some.

What ends the truce? Possibly a scourge of lampooning wall posters, gossip daubed in blue ink and stuck up at night all over town, purveying tales of infidelities and abortions and swindles. They seem to be what everybody knows, if not what everybody says. They contain no surprises, but they advertise scandal, and they bother everyone likely to be bothered by such publicity. A man is killed by a jealous husband, the priest worries, nagged by the town's respectable ladies, and the mayor imposes a curfew. The mayor's bullies kill a prisoner by mistake, shooting breaks out, men start to leave the town to join the guerrillas in the jungle. And still the invisible lampoonist continues his trivial, ruinous work, as if he had nothing to do with any of this.

As perhaps he hasn't, since García Márquez also proposes a quite different chain of causality. The town's dentist is passing round clandestine political leaflets, the prisoner who is killed was arrested for distributing them, and the shooting occurs because guns have been discovered beneath the floor of the barber's shop. Politics or gossip? The writer may be hesitating with his subject here, unsure which way to push it, but the kinship of lampoons and leaflets seems clear enough, and the relation of both of them to the writing of fiction is hard to miss.

The relation suggests not the claims of the imagination, as Vargas Llosa says of *In Evil Hour*, but the claims of mischief, the possible usefulness of making a disturbance. The claims of mischief are substantial, but also problematic, and they do imply an optimism about our ability to learn from disturbances which I suspect García Márquez doesn't have − or didn't have at this time. Certainly the fate of the town in the book is not encouraging, and the writer-lampoonist seems both exposed and helpless, terribly busy but really out of work. What if contemporary literature were closer to rumour and propaganda than to high art? Lightweight and dangerous rather than heavyweight and safe? Responsible writing might then seek to offer us practice in looking at our dangers.

The claims of mischief

Wittgenstein once said he could imagine a work of philosophy entirely composed of jokes. I think many jokes, if not made up of philosophy, are on intimate terms with it. Jokes are the opposite of what we think of as seriousness, and I don't wish to reclaim them, turn them into honest citizens. I do wish to suggest that they bear an interesting relation to seriousness, which is not simply that of an opposition; that they lightly or deviously or foolishly touch on topics that matter greatly to us; and that contemporary fiction, whether we think of the work of Beckett, Borges, Calvino, Queneau, Grass, Rushdie, Philip Roth, García Márquez or any number of others, is full of jokes in this sense. Criticism has not yet really found a language for these performances − the very notion of post-modernity tends to wither the most wonderful of gags − and keeps making contemporary writers mere earnest replicas or rejectors of their elders, as if they could succeed only by matching the criteria we happen to have in stock, or by questioning those same criteria.

García Márquez needs no explaining, he is the most accessible of writers, and I have not delved for buried or secret meanings in *One Hundred Years of Solitude*. I didn't have to, because the surface meanings of the book are prodigiously rich and varied, and full of invitations to comment. Indeed, García Márquez' very accessibility is, I think, quite unusual, since it depends on his simple presentation of a complex vision – a project quite different from simplification, from the reduction or abolition of complexity. I think it unlikely and undesirable that a writer should be conscious of all (or even most) of the meanings a reader may discover – although *conscious* is a question-begging term. In practice, writers often know everything critics claim to know, and a lot more. But they don't ordinarily put it into critical words, or into words at all; or they put it into stilted or archaic critical words, the lumbering language of a trade not their own. There are many dialogues of the deaf in this region. Henry James' Hugh Vereker was exceptional in inviting critics to look for a figure in his carpet, and even perhaps in believing there was a figure that a critic, of all people, might find. I haven't sought a single figure in the flying carpet of *One Hundred Years of Solitude*, but I have tried to trace some of the mischief's most marked weavings.

Chapter 2

Samples of style

> The facts of the life of a nation . . . are very strange indeed, and probably a half-magical idea is the quickest way to the truth.
>
> William Empson

Nadie supo a ciencia cierta cúando empezó a perder la vista. Todavía en sus últimos anos, cuando ya no podía levantarse de la cama, parecía simplemente que estaba vencida por la decrepitud, pero nadie descubrió que estuviera ciega. Ella lo había notado desde antes del nacimiento de José Arcadio. Al principio creyó que se trataba de una debilidad transitoria, y tomaba a escondidas jarabe de tuétano y se echaba miel de abeja en los ojos, pero muy pronto se fue convenciendo de que se hundía sin remedio en las tinieblas, hasta el punto de que nunca tuvo una noción muy clara del invento de la luz eléctrica, porque cuando instalaron los primeros focos sólo alcanzó a percibir el resplandor. No se lo dijo a nadie, pues habría sido un reconocimiento publico de su inutilidad. Se empeñó en un callado aprendizaje de las distancias de las cosas, y de las voces de la gente, para seguir viendo con la memoria cuando ya no se la permitieron las sombras de las cataratas. Más tarde había de descubrir el auxilio imprevisto de los olores, que se definieron en las tinieblas con una fuerza mucho más convincente que los volúmenes y el color, y la salvaron definitivamente de la vergüenza de una renuncia. En la oscuridad del cuarto podía ensartar la aguja y tejer un ojal, y sabía cúando estaba la leche a punto de hervir. Conoció con tanta seguridad el lugar en que se encontraba cada cosa, que ella misma se olvidaba a veces de que estaba ciega.

No one knew exactly when she began to lose her sight. Even in her later years, when she could no longer get out of bed, it seemed that she was simply defeated by decrepitude, but no one discovered that she was blind. She had noticed it before the birth of José Arcadio. At first she thought it was a matter of a passing debility and she secretly took marrow syrup and put honey on her eyes, but quite soon she began to realize that she was irrevocably sinking into the darkness, to a point where she never had a clear notion of the invention of the electric light, for when they put in the first bulbs she was only able to perceive the glow. She did not tell anyone about it because it would have been a public recognition of her uselessness. She concentrated on a silent schooling in the distances of things and people's voices, so that she would still be able to see with her memory what the shadows of her cataracts no longer allowed her to. Later on she was to discover the unforeseen help of odors, which were defined in the shadows with a strength that was much more convincing than that of bulk and color, and which saved her finally from the shame of admitting defeat. In the darkness of the room she was able to thread a needle and sew a buttonhole and she knew when the milk was about to boil. She knew with so much certainty the location of everything that she herself forgot that she was blind at times.   [216: 231]

This passage is characteristic of *One Hundred Years of Solitude* in many ways. We learn what people believe and know and do, but we don't hear them speak. García Márquez has said he uses dialogue sparingly because 'it doesn't ring true in Spanish', and we might say that the dialogue he does use doesn't even try to ring true — or rings only with the truth of epigram or summary. Speech in this novel tends to be repartee or wisecrack or memorable phrase, a means of framing or focussing a story but not of telling one. The narrative itself has a 'spoken' feel, in spite of what García Márquez sees as the gap between speech and writing in Spanish, but it achieves this by borrowing from talk or oral tradition a few structural habits — like casual syntax or a dependence on reported conversation — rather than by imitating a surface or a manner.

The sentences are simple and loosely connected — *very* loosely connected, since the *but* in the second sentence could easily be an *and*. The fourth sentence has the ribbon development of gossip, all in a rush, full of parataxis: 'At first she . . . and she . . . took . . . and put . . . but quite soon . . . to a point where . . . for when . . . she was only able . . .' This sounds like the linguistic custom of the community, or more precisely like a character thinking the way the community talks. The passage moves easily from the position of an informed third person ('No one knew . . . She did not tell anyone') to a perspective very much the character's own ('She began to realize . . . She forgot . . .'). The tenses of the verbs are straightforward, progressing generally (with one pluperfect) from the historic to the imperfect, as the condition being described settles in, *becomes* a condition. However, there are interesting oscillations in the temporal view, entirely typical of this book. The first sentence narrates the beginning of the condition, the second suddenly leaps to the end of the woman's life. The third returns to the time of her first noticing the symptoms, although the dating is open: it was before José Arcadio was born, but how long before? The next sentences then establish a steady time sequence which looks good for a long run but is mildly upset by the curious 'Later on she was to discover . . .' No narrative sense would have been lost if the text had read 'Later on she discovered. . .', so the disturbance seems gratuitous, some sort of game with time and meaning. In fact it is the prolongation of a stylistic habit, almost a signature in the book. I shall discuss this particular verbal form (*was to, había de*) in another chapter, and it will be enough here to say that it looks both forward and backward, points to a place where the future of the story will have become (what it always was) the past of the narrator and the present of the reader. The language, without breaking its stride or doing anything out of the ordinary, quietly confesses this odd transaction. For a moment we want to know who is speaking, who has this knowledge and would want to tip his hand in this way, but then we forget our question, because the effect is so slight, and the story calls.

The vocabulary of the passage is conventional but not faded, and has quite a wide range. It can accommodate familiar phrases like *a ciencia cierta, a escondidas, sin remedio*, which translate most easily into English as adverbs (exactly, secretly, irrevocably), and more literary terms like *tinieblas* and *sombras*, and metaphors like those of defeat by decrepitude or sinking into darkness, or an apprenticeship (nicely rendered as 'schooling' by Rabassa) in the distances of things. Apart from these mild metaphors there are no others, except for the beautifully simple one which illuminates the whole passage, and is set off by the relaxed literalness of the rest: 'see with her memory'. In fact this may be less a metaphor than a surprising transposition of faculties, a sort of synaesthesia. She doesn't just mentally see remembered things, as we all do, she makes memory do the actual work of sight.

There are plenty of material details in the passage − bed, syrup, honey, cataracts, smells, needle, milk − so that we are solidly located in a domestic world, although that world tends to be evoked as the result and object of human activity rather than as a settled scene or free-standing environment such as we find in so many nineteenth-century novels. There is no 'realism' here in that sense, not even 'magical realism'. The chief material fact in the passage, the arrival of electricity, is ambiguously present, because the central character can't really see the light. It has the improbable, historical and possibly irrelevant status of so many things in this book. It is a 'fact', but it feels like a figure, a metonymy − the phrasing 'nunca tuvo una noción muy clara', she never had a very clear idea, hinting at this riddle, since it discreetly mingles mental and optical vision. Similarly, the woman's forgetting that she is blind is presumably literal − she actually does forget at times − but feels like a metaphor for many occasions, a reminder that we have entered a realm where even the seemingly unforgettable can be forgotten.

It is not easy to describe the feeling this passage provokes, and perhaps we shouldn't try too hard, as long as we have the feeling. We are looking at Úrsula Iguarán de Buendía, matriarch of the line of the first family in Macondo. She has lost track of how old she is and has been complaining about the 'poor quality' of the time they are getting these days. She doesn't mean former times were better, only that there was more time then. Her age is a solitude, and her blindness is another. But to be blind and not known to be blind is to be unimaginably isolated and, in her case, strangely victorious. She doesn't tell her family about her blindness because she can't admit her uselessness, can't bear the shame of defeat, or more precisely, of renunciation, *renuncia*. But she is not useless and therefore would in any case be wrong to admit it, because she can see with her memory, and the text goes on beyond the passage given to show just how useful she is. She finds things others have lost because she knows their habits better than they do themselves, and because she spots every slight swerve in custom:

after some time she discovered that every member of the family, without realizing it, repeated the same path every day, the same actions, and almost repeated the same words at the same hour. Only when they deviated from meticulous routine did they run the risk of losing something.   [216–217: 231–232]

Úrsula is a sort of tropical Tiresias, who sees not the future but the stagnant present. We admire her dignity, smile at her subterfuges, but above all feel her unconfessed blindness as a source of pathos — the pathos of old age or disability or being left behind, but also more generally the pathos of any serious severance from our ordinary means of knowing the world. Úrsula's bravery and the narrator's unsentimental tone moderate this pathos but don't take it away. And yet Úrsula's memory produces real understanding. It is a form of historical imagination, and her methods of reconstruction may be even more necessary in less domestic circumstances. Seeing with the memory is one way, and in some instances the only way, of keeping a record.

Muchos años después, el niño había de contar todavía, a pesar de que los vecinos seguían creyéndolo un viejo chiflado, que José Arcadio Segundo lo levantó por encima de su cabeza, y se dejó arrastrar, casi en el aire, como flotando en el terror de la muchedumbre, hacia una calle adyacente. La posición privilegiada del niño le permitió ver que en ese momento la masa desbocada empezaba a llegar a la esquina y la fila de ametralladoras abrió fuego. Varias voces gritaron al mismo tiempo:
   — ¡Tírense al suelo! ¡Tírense al suelo!
Ya los de las primeras líneas lo habían hecho, barridos por las ráfagas de metralla. Los sobrevivientes, en vez de tirarse al suelo, trataron de volver a la plazoleta, y el pánico dio entonces un coletazo de dragón, y los mandó en una oleada compacta contra la otra oleada compacta que se movía en sentido contrario, despedida por el otro coletazo de dragón de la calle opuesta, donde también las ametralladoras disparaban sin tregua. Estaban acorralados, girando en un torbellino gigantesco que poco a poco se reducía a su epicentro porque sus bordes iban siendo sistemáticamente recortados en redondo, como pelando una cebolla, por las tijeras insaciables y

metódicas de la metralla. El niño vió una mujer arrodillada, con los brazos en cruz, en un espacio limpio, misteriosamente vedado a la estampida. Allí lo puso José Arcadio Segundo, en el instante de derrumbarse con la cara bañada en sangre, antes de que el tropel colosal arrasara con el espacio vacío, con la mujer arrodillada, con la luz del alto cielo de sequía, y con el puto mundo donde Úrsula Iguarán había vendido tantos animalitos de caramelo.

Many years later that child was still to tell, in spite of people thinking that he was a crazy old man, how José Arcadio Segundo had lifted him over his head and let himself be pulled away, almost in the air, as if floating on the terror of the crowd, toward a nearby street. The child's privileged position allowed him to see at that moment that the wild mass was starting to get to the corner and the row of machine guns opened fire. Several voices shouted at the same time:

"Get down! Get down!"

The people in front had already done so, swept down by the wave of bullets. The survivors, instead of getting down, tried to go back to the small square, and the panic became a dragon's tail as one compact wave ran against another which was moving in the opposite direction, toward the other dragon's tail in the street across the way, where the machine guns were also firing without cease. They were penned in, swirling about in a gigantic whirlwind that little by little was being reduced to its epicenter as the edges were systematically being cut off all around like an onion being peeled by the insatiable and methodical shears of the machine guns. The child saw a woman kneeling with her arms in the shape of a cross in an open space, mysteriously free of the stampede. José Arcadio Segundo put him down there at the moment he fell with his face bathed in blood, before the colossal troop wiped out the empty space, the kneeling woman, the light of the high, drought-stricken sky, and the whorish world where Ursula Iguarán had sold so many little candy animals.

[266: 283–284]

This passage opens with one of the novel's favourite phrases, and quickly moves to the signature tune of *was to, había de*. But our curiosity about who may be speaking in this way is now compounded by a double perspective in the character: the child is also a future old man. We are used to points within a fiction which explain how the story is possible, how a person comes to know what he knows, and this happens here. The child is lifted up by José Arcadio Segundo, and that is how he can see so well what he will remember and report. But the 'privileged position' is also an exposed one, and the effect is not to reassure us about knowledge but to make knowing seem risky, dangerously come by. We see the seer up in the air, unlikely to live long and for that reason unlikely to be believed if he does.

There is a grammatical third person in this passage ('the child was to tell. . .' 'the child saw. . .'), but very little sense of a narrative third person, of anyone other than the child grown old and still young. The call to get down, too late for some, is a grim linguistic joke: the people, persuaded by death, as the mention of *survivors* in the next sentence makes clear, have inadvertently, prematurely done as they were told. The language, as befits that of someone trying hard to make others see, is more overtly metaphorical than in the previous passage – dragons, a whirlwind, the machine gun fire as shears, the terror of the crowd as a river or flood. It is slightly repetitive (*ametralladoras, metralla, ametralladoras, metralla*), relaxed in its registers, shifting speedily from epicentre to onions; lyrically remembering the drought-stricken sky above the massacre. The chief metonymy in the passage is very clearly signalled, Úrsula's candy animals standing for everything Macondo will not know again. 'Puto mundo', the whorish world, is a swift intrusion of rage and baffled affection, perhaps the child/old man's, perhaps less specifically owned. It means something like: this world was shabby but it was ours, we were tired of it but we also loved it, and never thought it would end in this fashion – the sort of intimate effect a certain way of saying 'that bloody world' might get in English. Of course this world doesn't end, what ends is its innocence, which has somehow survived long civil wars, but can't survive the death of more than 3,000 unarmed protesters in the town square.

José Arcadio Segundo is later said to be the only survivor, but this must mean the only survivor of the purge which followed the massacre, or perhaps the only adult survivor. Even so the phrase reinforces the solitude of the child, invented purely so that he can see what no one will believe; half-forgotten even by the prose of the novel. Indeed, he and José

Arcadio Segundo both seem to die in this paragraph, because the light and the world go out, and the man's face is bathed in blood. Neither of them does die, but to survive in these conditions is to be a sort of ghost, hero and narrator of a hopelessly tall tale. If we wish to hear the tale, we must be prepared to hear what others can't or won't hear, and the task becomes especially important when the tall tales are true. By truth, here and elsewhere in this book, I don't mean anything transcendental or absolute, only the practical opposite of worldly lies and mystery: like the death of more than 3,000 people, denied by those who have an interest in denying it, and have the power to support their interest.

In order to talk to us, ghosts have to be trusted, and in Greek myth, for example, they have to be given blood to drink. We have moved now from the world Úrsula could establish in the darkness by memory and wit and smell, to a world, also evoked through Úrsula and her candy animals, which will not exist at all unless listeners accept the story of a narrator who seems not only unreliable but downright cracked, asserting what no one else can confirm. Úrsula doesn't see but manages; the child sees but becomes no one. Between these possibilities, between that chance and this risk, *One Hundred Years of Solitude* marks out the job it wants to give to fiction. The implication is that truth exists but needs fumbling for and may not be where we usually look. It can vanish altogether if we don't care for it, and apparently crazy truths are worth more than apparently documented lies. Unlikeliness is not a guarantee of truth, of course. All we can say is that likeliness may not be much of a guide in a region where disproportion, as García Márquez says, is part of reality. We may now be ready to approach the incredible Macondo.

Chapter 3

The history of paradise

This is the story of how we begin to remember.
Paul Simon

Situations

It would be absurd, and horribly dull, to try to summarize
One Hundred Years of Solitude, except as a rambling joke.
'I merely wanted', García Márquez said to Rita Guibert, 'to
tell the story of a family who for a hundred years did
everything they could in order not to have a son with a pig's
tail, and . . . ended up having one.' This is a good joke
because the pig's tail is both much worried about and really
a diversion. It is what the family is afraid of, and what awaits
it. But between the fear and its fulfilment the whole novel
takes place, and most characters don't think about the pig's
tail at all. It is a lure, an instance of what Roland Barthes
called 'a narrative enigma'. Well, it is also a sign of incest, but
that is a lure too, since the incest in the book, although always
hovering, is mainly metaphorical or merely flirted with.

Still, summaries apart, we do need a means of holding the
book in our minds, and we see at once that it is indeed 'the
story of a family', the prodigious Buendías; and even more
the story of a place, the human geography of the family's
fortunes.

José Arcadio Buendía, with whom our story begins, is
described as a young patriarch, and might be said to go even
further back into the Bible, since he is the first citizen of a sort
of paradise. It is an ambiguous paradise, far from perfect and
not available for easy nostalgia, but its loss, nevertheless,

24

means that much of *One Hundred Years of Solitude* reads like an elegy. From the start the tiny settlement of Macondo is offered to us as a version of Eden. 'The world', we read, 'was so recent that many things lacked names, and in order to indicate them it was necessary to point.' The polished stones in the clear river are 'white and enormous, like prehistoric eggs' [9:11]. There are twenty-odd mud and cane houses in the villages, homes of the twenty-odd founding families. The population soon grows to 300, but it is still a 'truly happy village' where no one is over thirty and no one has died [16:18]

Where is this Eden? If we draw a map based on the information given to us in the first two chapters of the novel, we get something like Map 1.

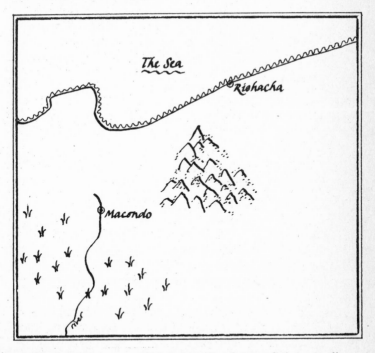

We have no way of knowing the shape of the coastline, but we know that the sea is to the north of Macondo; that a range of mountains separates Macondo from Riohacha; that Drake is supposed to have attacked Riohacha in the sixteenth century and hunted crocodiles there; that there are swamps to the south and west of Macondo; and that roads, towns and a sort of modernity can be found two days' travel to the west, 'on the other side of the swamp [39:43]. We hear of 'colonial coins' [10:12]; of 'authorities', a 'government', and a distant 'capital' [11: 13].

Northern Colombia, in which there is an 'ancient city' called Riohacha, looks something like Map 2.

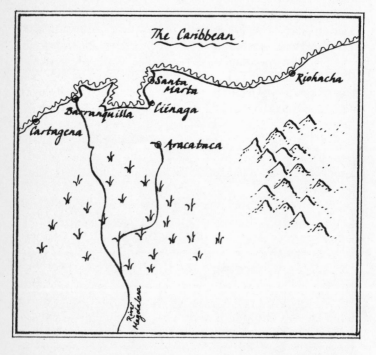

Macondo is the name of a banana plantation near Aracataca, García Márquez' birthplace, but this scarcely signifies, since it is now internationally famous as the name of a mythical community, the Latin American equivalent of Faulkner's Yoknapatawpha County. The point about the maps is not to

say that the setting of *One Hundred Years of Solitude is* Colombia — if García Márquez had wanted to name his country
he would have done so — only that its geography and history
are not different; that the imagined world has a real situation
in time and space. The analogy with Faulkner is exact in this
respect, I think. We are not going to find the town of Jeffer-
son on any map of Mississippi. But there isn't anywhere else
on earth it could be.

The recentness of this world turns out to be a metaphor, an
impression, and not a situation in time. The time indeed is
relatively late, very late if we are thinking of Eden: 'several
centuries' later than the sixteenth, and some 'three hundred
years' since Drake's incursions into the Spanish Main
[24:27]. An early expedition by the villagers discovers a suit
of rusty armour, complete with calcified skeleton; a later expedition leads them to a great Spanish galleon, stranded some
twelve kilometres from the sea, embedded among stones and
draped with orchids. The armour is said to be from the fif-
teenth century, which it could just be, since the northeastern
coastal region of South America, what is now Colombia and
Venezuela, was first visited by Europeans, with and without
armour, in 1499–1500. Santa Marta was founded in 1525;
Cartagena in 1533.

Do we *know* we are in the Americas? Even if we don't look
at the maps? We do if we are not desperate to see Macondo
as a never-never land or a universal allegory. García Márquez
is scrupulously quiet about large terms like nations and the
year of Our Lord. But he is precise about place names, days
of the week, months, seasons, political parties, peace treaties,
an accordion given to a musician by Sir Walter Raleigh. We
learn of the Spanish ancestry of the settlers. There are
Liberals and Conservatives. There is much importation of
fancy goods from Europe: furniture from Vienna, linen from
Holland, glassware from Bohemia. A civil war ends with the
peace of Neerlandia, which the history books (but not García
Márquez) tell us was signed in 1902. There are Indians in the
region, speaking their own prehispanic tongue, a people for
whom this world is not at all recent. When the settlers are said

to be 'the first mortals' [28: 31] to see the western slope of
the mountains they have crossed in their pioneering journey,
we need to understand the phrase, again, as a metaphor or
hyperbole, a figure for a feeling. They were the first mortals
of European descent, the new world was not empty, just empty of their kind. Even Eden is relative in this light, a glancing
joke (can one *arrive* in Eden?), and another Biblical reference
confirms this sense of mischief. The founders of Macondo
have travelled to a 'land no one had promised them' [27: 31].

García Márquez creates wide meanings by copious omis-
sions and by the use of specific but not local details. Colombia becomes a generic, legendary Latin America, a place of
innocence and isolation and charm, of high mountains and
rainy tropics and ash-coloured sea, but also of internal wars,
bureaucrats, booms, strikes, North American interventions,
and fits of fondness for the military. It is a sub-continent
carefully suspended between myth and the atlas, rather as the
name Baghdad, say, used to make Westerners feel they were
both in the Middle East and in the Arabian Nights. It feels recent because it keeps hiding from history. It is Eden not
because it is pristine and original, but because it has forgotten
the Fall. Or almost forgotten.

The settlers bring with them the very stories they hoped to
leave behind. The happy village is founded on remorse, since
José Arcadio Buendía killed a man who attacked his honour,
and whose ghost troubled his sleep and sent him journeying.
José Arcadio Buendía is above all struck by the *loneliness* of
the ghost, an early sounding of the theme which dominates
the book, and later, when the village is not quite so happy and
someone has died, the ghost finds his way to Macondo,
driven by a longing for the company of the living, and
oriented by Macondo's appearance on the 'motley maps of
death' [75: 80]. He is old now, his hair white and his gestures
uncertain, and José Arcadio Buendía is startled to learn that
'the dead also aged' [74: 80]. Perturbed by the contradictory
behaviour of time – it seems both static and changing – José
Arcadio Buendía loses all sense of temporal measurement,
and runs amok, frothing at the mouth, reverting to

what is described as 'a state of total innocence' [76: 82]. It is a haunted innocence, though, since he is also barking in a strange language which turns out to be Latin: the linguistic equivalent of finding the old armour or the Spanish galleon. José Arcadio Buendía has fallen into a past he didn't know was there. Certainly only a miracle could start a man speaking a language without learning it, but even miracles have implications. There is a similar implication in another splendid gag, worthy of Cervantes, which has José Arcadio Buendía, by dint of much watching of the sun and stars, and much work with his astrolabe, sextant and compass, discover for himself that the earth is round. The discovery is authentic, all his own, so foreign to his community that no one there believes him. But this new Columbus gets his chance only because his culture has forgotten the old one, and it is of course a lovely, dizzying touch to make a group of *Americans* forget Columbus.

Macondo's innocence is also an ignorance. Paradise is a refuge, a simplification of social existence, a form of solitude. There is another Fall. Progress arrives uninvited, propelled by its incapacity for leaving things alone. The distant government, for example, stretches out an unwelcome arm in the shape of a *corregidor* (chief magistrate), complete with six ragged soldiers, ordering all the houses in the village to be painted blue, 'in celebration of the anniversary of national independence' [56: 61]. Independence, the nation: the very history Macondo thought it had abandoned.

But the inhabitants of Macondo also reverse their escape themselves by seeking out the once excluded world. Even Úrsula Buendía, remorselessly sceptical about her husband's inquiries, orders a pianola for her new house, which in turn attracts an Italian pianola expert, who becomes a suitor to the girls of the family. José Arcadio Segundo tries to open up river communication for the town, and brings in its first and last boat, a log-raft loaded with French prostitutes. Aureliano Triste goes off to find his fortune and returns to Macondo with the railway, 'the innocent yellow train that was to bring so many ambiguities and certainties, so many pleasant and unpleasant moments, so many changes, calamities, and feelings of nostalgia to Macondo' [196: 210]. The railway indeed announces the whole modern world, with its electricity, movies, telephone, gramophones, cars.

What all this tells us is that haunted paradises come to an end just like their pure precursors. There is no hiding from history for long, and we know this from the very first sentence of the book, where we hear of violence before we hear of Eden. 'Many years later, as he faced the firing squad, Colonel Aureliano Buendía was to remember that distant afternoon when his father took him to discover ice' [9: 11]. *Discover* is *conocer*, to get to know what ice is, to see a piece of ice for the first time, exactly as José Arcadio Buendía discovers that the earth is round. Another name for innocence here is isolation, solitude: not knowing and not having what others know and have. It is a dubious privilege, but even so there is sadness in its cancellation. The *distant afternoon* is the time of the refuge, the tiny settlement and the clear river, and we learn at once that at least one of its inhabitants will find his way to a military rank and a death sentence. Much turbulent Latin American history hovers in that casual mention of the firing squad — in the casualness perhaps even more than in the mention. It is in exactly the same tone that the narrator, describing the founding of the village, alludes to the second civil war before we have heard of the first [28: 31].

In this paradise as in others knowledge is the serpent's bait, innocent enough in moderation but only to be had, it seems, in excess. In the early days a band of gypsies is Macondo's single connection to the wide world. They arrive every March, bringing with them what are described as 'new inventions' [9: 11] — new to Macondo, that is — like magnets, magnifying glasses, instruments of navigation, an alchemy set, false teeth. Their leader is a fat fellow with a beard and sparrow's hands and an 'Asiatic look that seemed to know what there was on the other side of things' [13: 15]. His name is Melquíades. One March, a fresh set of gypsies appears with the news that Melquíades is dead, and with rather different inventions: a mind-reading monkey, a machine that sews buttons and brings down fever, a poultice for killing time, and the ice Aureliano Buendía discovers in the book's first sentence. José Arcadio Buendía leads his two sons into a tent which is said to have belonged to King Solomon:

there was a giant with a hairy torso and shaven head, with a copper ring in his nose and a heavy iron chain on his ankle, watching over a pirate chest. When it was opened by the giant, the chest gave off a glacial exhalation. Inside there was only an enormous, transparent block with infinite internal needles in which the light of the sunset was broken up into colored stars.   [23: 25–26]

José Arcadio Buendía touches the ice, 'his heart filled with fear and jubilation at the contact with mystery', and solemnly announces, 'This is the great invention of our time' [23: 26].

José Arcadio Buendía's appetite for inventions is an appetite of the imagination. Even his apparently practical schemes, like finding gold with a magnet or making gold through alchemy, are really dabblings in disinterested science, quests for wonder – the chance of gain a mere mask or excuse for curiosity. And when José Arcadio Buendía and his men go exploring, they are seeking 'contact with the great inventions' [16: 19], as if they could modernize Eden without damage, as if they could import only wonder. What they find is the Spanish galleon.

There is more than a mild and amusing relativism here. What is new for some is old for others, but the inference points not simply to the variety of human experience but to the vagaries of historical time, and to the special meaning of innocence I mentioned a page or so back. 'We do not all inhabit the same time', Ezra Pound said, and García Márquez, later in this book, offers a concise and witty formulation of this theory:

time also stumbled and had accidents, and could therefore splinter and leave an eternalized fragment in a room . . .   [303: 322]

Certain South American Indians even now live in the Stone Age while we live in the Age of the Concorde. We ourselves have mental equipment, assumptions and values which largely belong to the nineteenth century, as if the twentieth century had not entirely happened to us yet. Terms like the Third World, concepts like backwardness or mental age, rest on the notion of splinterable time, and when, in this novel, the self-taught yet very learned Aureliano Babilonia grows up, he knows nothing of his own period, the early twentieth century, but has 'the basic knowledge of medieval man' [309: 328]

Macondo then is neither benighted nor blessed nor removed from time altogether. It is remote and contemporary, one of time's fragments, a place of temporal solitude. José Arcadio Buendía's wonderment at the ice and his brilliant personal discovery of the earth's roundness are both jokes on him and tributes to him, concrete forms of equivocation, rather like Don Quixote's courage when faced with lions which won't fight him. The lions are hungry and dangerous, but not in the mood for battle right now, so Quixote's quite genuine courage remains untested: his folly is heroic, but his heroism looks foolish. José Arcadio Buendía's intelligence and imagination are astounding but absurdly situated, and his innocence adds a further twist to the story. He doesn't even know that folly or heroism is in the offing.

Solitudes

The Spanish galleon the settlers find is beached out of its time and out of its element, and it hangs in the mind like an emblem of Macondo and the Buendía family, or rather of the kind of enchantment they suffer and embody:

Before them, surrounded by ferns and pale trees, white and powdery in the silent morning light, was an enormous Spanish galleon. Tilted slightly to the starboard, it had hanging from its intact masts the dirty rags of its sails in the midst of its rigging, which was adorned with orchids. The hull, covered with an armor of petrified barnacles and soft moss, was firmly fastened into a surface of stones. The whole structure seemed to occupy its own space, one of solitude and oblivion, protected from the blemishes of time and the habits of birds. Inside, where the expeditionaries explored with careful intent, there was nothing but a thick forest of flowers.   [18: 20–21]

The mood of this vision is oddly attractive and dislocated.
Commentators have naturally seized on the sentence beginning 'The whole structure seemed to occupy its own space, one
of solitude and oblivion. . .' This is, as Jacques Joset remarks
in his edition, the first mention of solitude in the book. We
have the words *oblivion, forgetting* and *forgetfulness* for
olvido, but here we really need something like *forgottenness*,
a state of abandonment or neglect which is not quite the
blankness of oblivion. It is true that the sentence allegorizes
the ship, and points to other magical spaces, like Melquíades'
room in the Buendía house, the place where time splinters and
leaves fragments. But the effect of the image is less logical
and discursive than allegory usually is, more like a moment
in a dream which trails criss-crossing meanings from waking life. The ship is piracy and conquest, a whole patch
of Spanish history. But it is also elegance and magic, a
release from the purposes of plunder and voyaging. The rags
of sail suggest a disaster, but the orchids look like a
carnival.

We are viewing a wonder and a freak, a sight at once ruined
and luxurious. It implies a human invasion of nature, and
nature's easy incorporation of the man-made. A whole tradition of Latin American fiction is evoked here, in a mixture of
homage and mischief − the tradition represented by Rivera's
La Vorágine, for instance, which ends with the words which
Carlos Fuentes has wittily taken as a motto for literature's
hitherto losing battle against geography: 'The jungle swallow-
ed them', 'se los tragó la selva'. But then the swallowing here
feels curiously benign; the humans have just slipped away,
become nature, the ship is a landscape. Solitude in this context seems to mean an enviable privacy, and being forgotten
might be a kind of historical grace. The 'forest of flowers'
insists on the sense of what I have called the refuge,
the expiry of noise and confusion. If we take these associa-
tions back to the Buendías and Macondo, we see some of the
attractions of solitude, and something of the immense appeal
of this haughty, eccentric and disorderly family; and we have, I
think, one of the secrets of the novel's extraordinary success: it

beautifully pictures the charm of what we are not ordinarily supposed to find charming.

And yet. The galleon is *only* beautiful, and it is lost. It is stranded, sterile, and has no connection to continuing human life. It is isolated – a word which lacks the proud ring of *solitude* – and being forgotten, like being ignorant, is an equivocal grace. When García Márquez, receiving the Nobel Prize, spoke of the solitude of Latin America – that was the title of his acceptance speech – he meant its difference, its strangeness to others, and the failure of supposedly friendly countries to offer concrete support to its aspirations. It is true that he also took pride in what he saw as the source of this difference, the extravagant unlikeliness of much of life in Latin America, but this is precisely the reverse side of the same coin. Solitude is like progress: one always has too much or too little.

It is worth pausing over the word. *Soledad* is an alluring, mournful, much-used Spanish noun, suggesting both a doom and a solace, a flight from love but also from lies, a claim to dignity which is also a submission to neglect. *Loneliness* has some of this flavour, but only some. *Soledad* is part of a culture which calls its streets paradise or bitterness or disenchantment; and gives girls names like Virtues, Sorrows and Mercies. Soledad is itself a girl's name, and the name of Octavio Paz's Mexican labyrinth. *Soledades* is the title of one of the most famous poems in the Spanish language, Góngora's evocation of a pastoral shipwreck.

The word haunts the book, attaching itself to virtually every character. It is an 'air', an appearance which permits all Aureliano's sons to be identified instantly as his [190: 204], 'a look of solitude that left no doubt as to the relationship' [137: 146]. When members of the family are not solitary but gregarious they seem strange, defectors or mutants, and even then we hear of the 'bitter solitude' [237: 254] of the jolly Aureliano Segundo's revels; and his daughter Meme, a cheerful, sociable girl who hangs out with the newly resident Americans and invites sixty-eight schoolmates and four nuns to stay with her in Macondo over the holidays, finds her own solitude when she is very young. Her lover is shot and crippled for life, and she never speaks again, dying many years later in a convent in Cracow. In her happy days, we are told, she 'did not yet show the solitary fate of the family', 'no revelaba todavía el sino solitario de la familia' [227: 243] – that is, she didn't show any sign of her share in such a fate. The *yet* is cruel and touching, since it knows what she doesn't know, and the *fate* seems horribly accidental. Her lover is injured and their love exposed because he is mistaken for a chicken thief. It is Meme's fate, perhaps, or at least her character, that she should respond to her loss by shutting herself away in silence, but her solitude is only a fragile and disturbing compound of bad luck and stoicism. It is predetermined merely in the sense that it is what the novelist has decided is going to happen to her. García Márquez' use of this kind of textual fate is quite elaborate, and I shall return to it.

There are individual solitudes which are not the mark of the family or of the writer's conspiracy against his characters but responses to particular, troubling experiences: sexual initiation is a 'fearful solitude' [31: 35]; the possibility of fatherhood makes a man 'anxious for solitude' [35: 39]. Certain characters, like Aureliano and Amaranta Buendía, actually seem to incarnate solitude, and I shall look at them more closely in later chapters. Incest too, the great family terror and temptation, is an aspect of the theme, a refusal of the world of others, of the outside. But for the moment I want only to insist on the theme's richness and range, and to defend it against a particular simplification, which is that of many critics but also García Márquez' own.

Two instances help here. Rebeca Buendía, after an unhappy love and a tumultuous but contented marriage, becomes a stern and lonely widow, hidden away in her house, and entirely forgotten by Macondo, until someone stumbles on her, as if she were rusty armour or a Spanish galleon. She is said in her later years to have gained 'the privileges of solitude', which are contrasted to the 'false charms of pity' [194: 208 – 'los privilegios de la soledad/los falsos encantos de la misericordia]. Better to be alone and uncomplaining than to enjoy the promiscuous pity of others. We recognize a version of Meme's reaction to her grief. There is arrogance in such a posture, of course, but there is also dignity, and much moral authority. The privileges of solitude are not an illusion – and are certainly not to be spirited away by any sort of well-meaning sermon about companionship.

The other instance is even deeper. There is an ancient rivalry between Rebeca and Amaranta. They first fell out, or rather committed themselves to a scarcely spoken but implacable and enduring enmity, over Pietro Crespi, the Italian pianola expert. Amaranta discovers shortly before her death at a fairly advanced age that her feelings have ended neither in hatred nor in love but in 'the measureless understanding of solitude', 'la comprensión sin medidas de la soledad' [244: 260]. Grammatically the phrase could mean that solitude is what is understood, and it is true that the understanding concerns the solitary Rebeca. But the context clearly suggests the measureless understanding which solitude can give, which is the portion, or may be the portion, of those who are truly dedicated to solitude, like the Buendías. It is not an understanding that many of them reach, but the interesting implication lies in the moral possibility: solitude is a way of losing others and the world, but may also be an austere way of finding them. It was in just this sense that Proust spoke of books as the work of solitude and the children of silence.

As I have suggested, García Márquez himself is inclined to moralize this issue in a rather narrow way. 'The Buendías', he said in an interview, 'were incapable of loving and this is the key to their solitude and their frustration. Solitude, I believe, is the opposite of solidarity.' Elsewhere he has insisted that this is 'a political concept: solitude considered as the negation of solidarity.' It is true that the attraction of solitude, or quietism, is very dangerous, and especially for politically disaffected or despairing Latin Americans. And it is true that the Buendías are a family of monsters. But they are tremendously appealing monsters, and we can't dissipate their appeal by pretending we don't feel it – as García Márquez himself must have felt it. To say that the Buendías are incapable of loving is to travesty all the tenderness and torment and longing that abound in the book, and to muffle all kinds of differences among the characters. The Buendías have a hard time loving anyone. They get tangled in their pride, and they are amazingly stubborn. But this is not a moral or political verdict, or material for a slogan. It is what the novel is made of. García Márquez comments that he is 'not very good at these theorizings, which in my case are always *a posteriori*'. Or not quite always *a posteriori*, since we also find such theorizings, albeit quite rarely, in the novel itself. These attempts are invariably intelligent and interesting, but generally unavailing. The characters and events slip away, not because they are independent of their author − their place in the plot sees to that − but because they are, in most cases, richer than his formulas for them. This is particularly true, as we shall see, of Colonel Aureliano Buendía. Ideas may slip away too, because they are more complex in their concrete, dramatized form than they are when construed for argument. The Spanish galleon occupies a space of solitude and oblivion, but it is also a material memory, a recall to history, a lingering of the past in the present. It waits in the jungle like a destiny.

Sleep and forgetting

Paradise can be translated as solitude, and solitude, in this novel, suggests a lapse of memory. But what is forgotten is not necessarily dead, it may be mislaid or repressed. And even if dead, it may not be buried. When the unsettled past is refused by conscious thought, it often returns as a set of spectres − which is one reason for the multiplicity of ghosts in *One Hundred Years of Solitude*. They walk in these pages 'like the materialization of a memory' [309: 328] − because they *are* a materialization of memory, of a memory which has been denied or distanced, like the Latin language or a lost and found ship. The image is reversed, the ghosts quite plainly made figurative, when Rebeca is said to have 'found peace in that house where memories materialized through the strength of implacable evocation and walked like human beings through the cloistered rooms' [142: 152]. The whole novel is an evocation of this kind, since the Buendías are consigned to oblivion *in* the story, but resurrected *by* the story, remembered as often as the story is told.

Of course this story itself could be lost, or not have been told in the first place. We can see with the memory, as Úrsula Buendía does; but there are blindnesses of memory too, and all feats of remembering have to be set against this risk, as lights are held up against an always possible darkness. If there is one thing worse than the traffic of unquiet ghosts, it could well be the entire absence of ghosts, memory's utter abolition. The risk is notably dramatized in an early chapter, where the whole of Macondo finds itself unable to sleep, and consequently unable to remember.

The village has turned into a lively town, with Arab traders and new houses and musical clocks. Two Indians, brother and sister, now work for the Buendías. They have left their home region because of a 'plague of insomnia' there [40: 44], and this magical disease, reported like everything else in *One Hundred Years of Solitude* as if it were the most natural thing in the world, now smites the family and the town. At first people are quite pleased. They don't sleep but they don't feel tired, and there is plenty to do. 'This way we can get more out of life', José Arcadio Buendía happily says [45: 50]. But the disease insidiously develops toward 'a more critical manifestation: a loss of memory':

When the sick person became used to his waking state, the memories of his childhood began to fade, then the names and notions of things, and finally people's identities and even consciousness of his own being, until he was sunk in a kind of idiocy without a past.
[46: 50]

The inhabitants of Macondo soon start to long for sleep because they miss their dreams even before they miss their past, and José Arcadio Buendía begins to study the 'infinite possibilities of forgetting' [48: 53]. Aureliano thinks of a temporary stay against the damage. Every object is marked with its name – table, chair, clock, door, wall, bed, saucepan, cow, goat, pig, hen, banana – and in time with a note about its use — 'This is the cow. She needs to be milked every morning so that she will produce milk, and the milk must be boiled in order to be mixed with coffee to make milky coffee . . .' [49: 53]. At the entrance to the town a sign says MACONDO, and in the main street a larger sign says GOD EXISTS. Of course these measures will help only as long as people remember the alphabet. 'Thus they went on living in a reality that was slipping away, momentarily captured by words, but which would escape irremediably when they forgot the values of the written letters' [49: 53]. This sounds like a situation imagined by Borges, but only because Borges has caught so well the spectral, vanishing quality of so much of what is called reality in Latin America. 'Only the mist is real', Octavio Paz says in a poem.

Macondo does manage to quarantine itself and to stop the disease from spreading; in an imaginative inversion of the old practice connected with leprosy the town asks visitors to carry a bell signalling that they are healthy. And luckily, before forgetfulness takes over completely, the gypsy Melquíades returns from the dead, recognizes the illness for what it is, and supplies an antidote. The people of Macondo are able to celebrate 'the reconquest of memory' [50: 55].

Here as elsewhere in *One Hundred Years of Solitude* there is so much deadpan mischief in the writing that any act of interpretation is likely to seem pretty elephantine. I am sure that the chief connection between sleeplessness and forgetting is that there isn't one. Nonsense is precious and should not be recklessly converted into meaning on all occasions. Even so, I can't shake off the feeling of a subtly implied logic here, a sense that confirms rather than quarrels with the nonsense. Sleep is the means of memory, it seems. The past can accumulate only in the apparent forgetfulness of the night. If we were always awake, the time would always be the present. Or more crudely, if we can't forget, we can't remember. This is partly a truism, of course, a mere statement of what the word *remember* means; but it may also be an insight into quite particular fears, a specification of the tightrope that needs to be walked. The *totally* forgotten would no longer be forgotten, it would be nothing, it would have entered oblivion, a meaning the Spanish word *olvido* includes, as we have seen. Macondo is trying to forget history. The galleon and the armour, the Indians, the return of the dead Prudencio Aguilar and the dead Melquíades, are points where the enterprise fortunately fails. The insomnia plague is a figure for the possible and terrible *success* of the enterprise, for what its success would actually mean. There is a forgetting which allows memory to accumulate, unspied on; and there is a forgetting which takes memory away, along with everything else that matters. Time itself is the repository of history; and also an insomnia plague. The final wind which erases Macondo is a materialization of oblivion, the plague's last triumph, mitigated only by the precarious memory game of writing.

Chapter 4

Writers and magicians

> The great city will be quite desolate
> Of its inhabitants not one will remain.
>
> Nostradamus

Memories of the future

Writing is a form of seeing with the memory (although it is other things as well), and it pursues this activity by finding the future in the past, retracing the road of hindsight. All historical narratives do this to some degree, could scarcely manage without it, but the discovery of pointed promises is also something of a trick: an optical illusion which answers a real need, what Wallace Stevens would call a necessary fiction. García Márquez' vivid display of the need and the trick centres on the notion of destiny and some interestingly related verbal forms.

In the first sentence of *One Hundred Years of Solitude* we hear not only of ice and a firing squad and a rank, but of a future act of memory: 'Colonel Aureliano Buendía was to remember'. In the first chapter alone we are told that José Arcadio Buendía's sons 'were to remember for the rest of their lives' the solemnity with which he announced his discovery that the earth was round [12: 14]; that Aureliano 'was to remember for the rest of his life' Melquíades as he was one hot afternoon telling his fantastic stories [13: 15]; that the smell of a spilt chemical 'would stay for ever' in Úrsula's mind [13: 16]. José Arcadio Buendía himself 'would have liked to invent a memory machine' to register all the attractions the gypsies bring [22: 24]. And when, still in this first chapter, a verb of memory appears with a negative, the effect is both shocking and temporary: 'Úrsula did not remember' the intensity of the child Aureliano's gaze; did not remember it, that is, until three years later, when she would remember it for good [20–21: 23].

'Many years later. . .' these are not only the first words of the novel but a constant refrain in it, literally or in related forms. This town thoroughly cut off from past and present is haunted by the future. The narrative keeps getting ahead of itself, rather like that of Serenus Zeitblom in Thomas Mann's *Dr Faustus*, except that in this case there is not even a simulated clumsiness, only the unresisted invasion of the immediate story by later knowledge, as if neither town nor text had any defence against the narrator's privileged information. 'The cemetery still smelled of gunpowder for many years after . . .' [122: 131]; 'The man . . . lost his serenity for ever . . . and years later was cut to pieces by a train after he had fallen asleep on the tracks' [174: 186–187]. 'A *few* years later', 'many years *before*': temporal variants on the key phrase reinforce the porous effect in the narrative – as if time had only shaky partitions, as if moments could only trickle into other moments.

But this is a narrative *effect*, the way narrator and reader experience events which the characters have to take differently. Or rather, it is the way events add up for the characters when they see their own stories, when they have become a story for themselves, although there is a paradox here. In spite of the frequency of verbs for remembering, attached to most of the characters at one time or another, we don't see the difference their remembering makes. They are said to remember, and that is all – as if the narrator needed them to share his interest in memory but couldn't get them to act on it.

As my examples have already suggested, the novel is crowded with the idiom *was to, había de*, which looks, in Spanish and in English, like a tense of the verbs *haber* and *to be*, but is actually an interesting usage available in both past and present tenses of those verbs. Its function in French and German, for example, is picked up by *devoir* and *sollen*. It has the simple meaning of a plan or an arrangement – we are to have to dinner tonight, we were to have dinner last night − and is used in this way in *One Hundred Years of Solitude*. But its more intricate application suggests an appointment which could not have been missed, an affair which just was to be (or not to be); a fate, what was in the script, a memory of what would become the future.

Of course García Márquez didn't invent the idiom, and must have stumbled quite intuitively on its extraordinary usefulness for him. But his casual-seeming insistence on it may amount to a modest patent, a real discovery of the already known, since it displays so clearly our need to find the future tucked away in our past, and the readiness with which language delivers just this message, lets us see the story lurking in the mere litter of old events. García Márquez's trick is to pretend, and to allow us to pretend, that there is no difference between the two common meanings of the idiom: we assume without thinking very hard that there is something fateful about mere arrangements, but also, with a little help from our author, that there is something merely arranged about fate. The idiom can also be used for equivocations, like those of the witches in *Macbeth*. We are told of the grace and sense of responsibility a very young girl 'was always to have' [78: 84], the *was to* and the *always* both seeming to guarantee a long story. The story turns out to be distressingly short, a foiling of the apparent prediction: the girl dies within a year, *always* meant only the brief term of her life.

The apparent destiny here is not determinism but only hindsight; as a student of mine, Jackie Finlay, elegantly put it, 'all is predetermined, not because it has been predicted, but because it has already happened'. A novel's plot, highlighted in this way, is the perfect means of representing a familiar superstition (perhaps there really is a conspiracy of design around us, a malign or divine scenario) as well as the often unconfessed power of the author, who in this respect at least is always a god, master/mistress of a scenario merely suffered by the characters. Destiny thus seems quite plausible and remains rather fragile; manages to look like a reasonable way of making sense of events and also like a mere textual mirage, a manner of telling the same story twice.

The firing squad in the novel's opening sentence plays the same game even more clearly. It seems to be a dramatic early specification of Aureliano's end, and we read the sentence as saying that the ice was among his last memories. This is true. He thought of the ice and the distant afternoon just before he died; but he died of old age, having been rescued from the firing squad long before. It is also true that he thought of the ice as he faced the firing squad, so there is nothing false about the sentence at all, except the inference we are undoubtedly most tempted to draw. The firing squad is a prophecy both fulfilled and thwarted; what awaits Aureliano but not what kills him; and an image of how the novel works, an amusing narrative metaphor. I should add that the narrator goes out of his way to call the firing squad Aureliano's destiny [51: 56], which it is − it is just not as final as we usually think destinies have to be. It is *only* a destiny: one of the things that were to happen. The very concept of destiny is emptied of its implication of doom.

There are other firing squads in the book, including those that Aureliano himself sets up during the civil wars, and other condemned men do not escape. When the threatening phrase is repeated, and applied to Aureliano's unlovely nephew Arcadio − 'a few months later, facing the firing squad, Arcadio was to relive. . .' [104: 112] − the prediction is quite accurate and there is no rescue. The ice appears at his execution not as a childhood memory but as the coldness of death itself, an 'icy hardness' in the nostrils [111: 119]. García Márquez' implication seems to be that prophecies can be wrong but are quite often right − especially when they concern events which have already happened. As Pascal said, if error was *always* error it would be a form of truth.

With these baffled and rewarded guesses in our minds, along with the tune and rhythm of those repeating phrases, we can see the point of the modulation which opens the second half of the book. The twin sons of the executed Arcadio begin a new era in Macondo, full of echoes and alterations of the old one. 'Years later on his deathbed,

Aureliano Segundo was to remember the rainy afternoon in June when he went into the bedroom to meet his first son' [162: 174]. To meet is *conocer*, the same word as for the gypsies' ice, and it is afternoon again. But there is no military rank here, and no firing squad. There is a child instead of a curiosity, the father sees the son instead of the father taking the son to see something, and there is a promised death in bed. This is a world of peace and progress, although it turns out to be no great improvement on the world of war – more like a reshuffle, with a corresponding loss of energy. The firing squad itself returns in the story of Aureliano Segundo's twin, José Arcadio Segundo. As a child he asks to be taken to see an execution, and 'for the rest of his life he would remember (*recordaría*, a conditional this time) the livid flash of the six simultaneous shots and the echo . . . and the sad smile and perplexed eyes of the man being shot . . .' [165: 177]. The man is still smiling when he is dead, and José Arcadio Segundo is sure the body is being buried alive, and takes against the military because of this experience. He later becomes a union leader, and an important figure in the strike against the banana company; the political heir of the Colonel Aureliano Buendía who 'organized thirty-two armed uprisings and . . . lost them all' [97: 104]. José Arcadio Segundo is a survivor of a massacre of more than 3,000 strikers, a new kind of ghost, as we have seen. The double take in the imagery here is very nimble. The firing squad is no longer the hero's destiny, or even a part of it; it is what he goes to see in place of the ice. History repeats itself, not as farce, but as sideshow. And yet the spectator's role, the merely watched execution, finally take the boy further into history than the colonel ever got. José Arcadio Segundo remembers, he was to remember, not a curiosity or a fabulous invention, but a human horror.

García Márquez' most explicit and most dizzying play with the idea of destiny occurs in the story of Aureliano's son Aureliano José. This young man, we are told, 'was destined' to live happily with a girl called Carmelita Montiel, to be the father of three children, and to die of old age in his wife's affectionate arms [139: 149]. Unfortunately he is shot in a political squabble before any of this can happen. Even destiny's plans go awry. And yet:

The bullet that entered his back and shattered his chest had been directed by a wrong interpretation of the cards. Captain Aquiles Ricardo, who was really the one destined to die that night, did indeed die, four hours before Aureliano José.   [139: 149]

Aquiles Ricardo, the man who kills Aureliano José, manages to meet his own destiny by getting shot himself, and indeed by dying earlier than his unscheduled victim. But he also ruins Aureliano José's destiny in the process, turns it into a mere dream, an option not taken up. Circumstance here, like Pascal's error, gets only part of the story straight; kills the right man but also kills the wrong man. Pilar Ternera, Aureliano José's mother, has foreseen his death in the cards – has foreseen, that is, not his pleasant destiny but what was in fact going to occur. But then it seems to have occurred, bewilderingly, *because* she foresaw it – this is what 'directed by a wrong interpretation of the cards' means. She has cruelly misread his fortune, and the misreading has cruelly come true. There is a beautifully casual and mournful extension of this movement when poor Carmelita Montiel, whose destiny has also just evaporated, and whose only function in the novel is to be the happiness Aureliano José so narrowly missed, is said to find the cards of her future blank [140: 149]. She has only cancelled hopes.

The idea of a misreading of the cards creeping out into the world of events is quietly suggested here – and indeed the whole scene reflects philosophical playfulness rather than a developed theory of destiny. But the lethal misreading does serve to underline the role of interpretation in these matters. It is scarcely a metaphor to say that interpretations can kill, in and out of literature, and the sad joke here is to make destiny a happy abstraction and a mother's fear for her son a brutal historical presage.

Aureliano José's destiny is what was supposed to happen to him, an exact enactment of the *was to* formula. What did happen was . . . what happened, mere life. A destiny, we may say, is a project or an interpretation; life either takes it or leaves it. Fate is what actually happens, read in retrospect as if it had to happen. García Márquez uses the words fairly interchangeably, but the two meanings are clear, and both words lend a recognizable shape to events. What is subtly hinted at in this novel is that such shapes are both horribly tempting and perfectly consoling, in their morbid and elegant way. Man would rather choose nothingness than have nothing to choose, Nietzsche says; and viewers of horror movies would rather have the devil for an explanation than no explanation at all. A century or so of turbulent isolation is what happened, the raw recent history of Latin America. One hundred years of solitude is a destiny.

Melquíades' manuscripts

The hundred years of the novel's title echo the prophetic *Centuries* of Nostradamus, a sixteenth-century French astrologer and doctor distinguished for his work during outbreaks of plague, and repeatedly mentioned in the text. A hundred years is a long time, a mythical time, an unimaginable time − like that of the sideshow announced by the second set of gypsies, in which a woman is to be decapitated every night for 150 years [35: 39]. García Márquez may also be thinking of the Hispanic proverb which says that a thief who robs a thief gets a hundred years of pardon, 'ladrón que roba a ladrón/tiene cien años de perdón'. The attraction of this association is that it makes a hundred years a kind of lease, an inverted legal sentence; and a judicial verdict is what we read in the last line of the book, as the full title impressively unfurls:

because races condemned to one hundred years of solitude did not have a second opportunity on earth.   [360: 383]

Most important, a hundred years is the scope and term of Melquíades' manuscripts, a prophecy designed to serve as a past, a kind of occluded and externalized memory, everything the family ought to remember but won't. It is a destiny in the sense I have been trying to describe, but it is also better than a destiny, because it is right. It picks up and hides away, we might say, the promises of remembering the narrator keeps making on the characters' behalf. Colonel Aureliano Buendía was to remember the ice, and he did. Melquíades' history would remember even if Aureliano didn't; and it can report both Aureliano José's happy destiny and his sudden death on the street. And since it is in code, and not understood, it can do all this without interfering with the characters' experience or freedom. The last Aureliano knows that predictions need to be coded, 'so that they won't defeat themselves' [339: 360 – Rabassa's version has the meaning upside down here, converting 'ciphering' into 'deciphering']. Melquíades' text can be read only when the story is over, or about to end. One hundred years also means 'too late'.

Aureliano Segundo tries to read the manuscripts but can't – 'The letters looked like clothes hung out to dry on a line and they looked more like musical notation than writing' – and the ghost of Melquíades explains that a hundred years have to pass before they can be understood [164–165: 176–177 – Rabassa again mistakes the sense here: it is the manuscripts which need to be one hundred years old, not the future reader]. Much later, close to the end of the spell, Melquíades appears to the last Aureliano and asks him if he knows what language the manuscripts are written in. He does, and Melquíades tells him where to find the relevant primer. When his tiny child is dragged off by ravening ants, Aureliano grasps at last the full meaning of the once obscure text:

It was the history of the family, written by Melquíades, down to the most trivial details, one hundred years ahead of time. He had written it in Sanskrit, which was his mother tongue, and he had encoded the even lines in the private cipher of the Emperor Augustus and the odd ones in a Lacedemonian military code. The final protection . . . was based on the fact that Melquíades had not put events in the order of man's conventional time but had concentrated a century of daily episodes in such a way that they coexisted in one instant.
[359: 381–382]

As critics have suggested, Melquíades' organization of

narrative time recalls Borges' story 'The Aleph', where a
similar trick is performed for space (the Aleph is 'the place
which contains, clearly distinguished, all places on earth, seen
from all angles'); and the story of the man reading his own
story, prisoner of another's text, remembers Borges' 'The
Circular Ruins'. It helps to be reminded that we are fairly far
from realism here. By this I mean we don't have to rack
our brains looking for plausible explanations of Melquíades'
exotic codes, magical methods of composition or multiple
deaths. *One Hundred Years of Solitude* presents a world
neither of hard fact nor of embraced superstition, but a world
where the imaginary and the figurative are seriously enter-
tained and not visibly discriminated against. We don't need
to ask how Melquíades knows so precisely what he knows,
but we can ask what his knowledge means, what it is doing
in the book. Melquíades foresees the ins and outs of what I
have called the history of paradise, that is, both what it
reveals and what it hides. His mentality shadows all the prophetic tenses in the book, all the future memories, all the narrator's temporal indiscretions, all the glimpses of destiny and
the multiple, irregular structure of time.

Colonel Aureliano Buendía, returning from the wars, is
astonished by the way his town has aged. 'What did you expect?' his mother says, 'Time passes.' 'So it does', Aureliano
replies, 'but not as much as that', 'Así es, pero no tanto' [114:
123]. Later Úrsula finds herself having the same conversation
with José Arcadio Segundo, and in a reversal of roles, echoes
the now dead colonel's thought. But as she does so she feels
her echo and her agreement are wrong, that time doesn't pass
but just goes round [291–292: 310]. Of course it does both.
It comes back and it grows old, and the repeated conversation
is itself a witty instance of what it discusses: it is the same and
not the same the second time around. Pilar Ternera, taught
by 'a century of playing cards and experiences', that is a century of telling fortunes and of living and watching them,
understands with impeccable clarity that:

the history of the family was an interlocking system [*un engrenaje*,
an arrangement of cogwheels] of irreparable repetitions, a turning

wheel that would have gone on spinning into eternity were it not for the progressive and irremediable wearing of the axle. [343: 364]

Irreparable repetitions is wonderfully precise. The future can easily be foreseen in such a world, because the basic patterns are firmly set, and the repertory of character and gesture is quite limited. That is in part what a family means: a suit of marked cards, a smallish fund of possible combinations. But then the future has an end, winds down and dies; the repetitions themselves one day stop repeating. And there are surprises, openings and twists in the plot, failures of destiny to get its way, and for this reason the vision is not incompatible with human freedom. In a thoroughly determined world García Márquez' concept of an avoidable destiny could only be an illusion, not a good joke or a surprise movement of plot.

It has often been suggested that Melquíades' manuscripts *are* the novel we are reading, and it has also been suggested, on rather trivial grounds, that they can't be. To insist on the texts being identical is to miss Melquíades' fictional status and to overlook all kinds of questions: who fished the work out of the destruction of Macondo and produced this Spanish version for us? Above all it is to disregard the linear, successive experience of reading this or any other novel. Melquíades has magically concentrated his century of events into an instant as a *protection*, a means of keeping knowledge from his characters and saving them from knowledge. What we are reading is unprotected, consecutive prose – or a prose protected only by its scarcely visible irony. I think we can agree that the *contents* of the manuscripts and the novel may be the same, or at least that there is no good reason for them to be very different; that the novel's narrator, while making all necessary concessions to conventional time and the business of narrative, alludes to Melquíades' perspective whenever he can. We can even agree that the novel aspires to the condition of Melquíades' manuscripts, as Pater suggested all art aspires to the condition of music.

García Márquez has said that his own sense of time was 'completely transformed' by a sentence in Virginia Woolf's *Mrs Dalloway*, read when he was twenty. 'I saw in a flash the whole process of decomposition of Macondo and its final destiny.' The sentence in question is this:

> But there could be no doubt that greatness . . . was passing, hidden, down Bond Street, removed only by a hand's-breadth from ordinary people who might now, for the first time and last, be within speaking distance of the majesty of England, of the enduring symbol of the state which will be known to curious antiquaries, sifting the ruins of time, when London is a grass-grown path and all those hurrying along the pavement this Wednesday morning are but bones with a few wedding rings mixed up in their dust and the gold stoppings of innumerable decayed teeth.

With hindsight, or with *One Hundred Years of Solitude* in our heads, we can see the connections: a secret significance, guessed at and missed, close by and far away; the details of Bond Street and Wednesday and wedding rings and teeth caught up in a far future of ruins; above all, the sudden sense of a later time full of relics of what is now the present, the imagination of different events as if they all 'coexisted in one instant'. The greatness that is passing in *Mrs Dalloway* is an important personage in a car, but 'whether . . . Queen, Prince, or Prime Minister nobody knew'. The sentence after the quotation looks to the ruins for revelation: 'The face in the motor car will then be known.'

This is where García Márquez parts company with Woolf. For him, the equivalent of the face in the motor car will never be known, but can be guessed at with different sorts of scruple and success. It seems clear that Melquíades' manuscripts are destroyed with Macondo, where not even wedding rings and gold stoppings remain, and the place is entirely 'exiled from the memory of men' [360: 383]. From their memory, but not from their imaginative reach. The novel we read is a brilliant, impossible reconstruction of Melquíades' lost history, rather like the footfalls that sound in Eliot down the passage which we did not take: 'My words echo/Thus, in your mind'. The novel conjures up what was once predicted but cannot now be read or remembered, a fiction which is now the only history there is. It has no authority for the truth it offers (except what Thomas Pynchon calls imaginative anxiety or historical care), but insists on its truthfulness all the same, because, as García Márquez has said, following Stendhal, 'lies are more serious in literature than in real life', and 'you can't imagine or invent just whatever you fancy'. You can imagine or invent all kinds of implausible stuff, because figures of speech are not a problem, and the literalization of figures of speech, as if in some kind of tropical homage to the Marx Brothers, is a favourite technique of this writer's. What you can't do is abandon the imagined truth for mere whimsy: the imagined truth may be all the truth we have.

Macondo is doubly fictional: because it is a place in a novel, and because even if it weren't it would have to be invented, like the past in Latin America — lost, exiled, a prey to the imagination at best and oblivion at worst. Borges' incomparable story 'Tlön, Uqbar, Orbis Tertius' suggests that 'already in our memories a fictitious past occupies the place of another, of which we know nothing for certain — not even that it is false'. We have to trust the writer to resurrect Melquíades' history, not subvert it or rewrite it, and again there are no guarantees. 'I think the novel is reality represented through a secret code', García Márquez says, 'a kind of conundrum about the world'. This code — metaphorical where Melquíades' is literal — is a shield and a necessity, a sign of the dreamwork of art, not a lie or an evasion. The most striking thing perhaps about García Márquez's code as we see it in *One Hundred Years of Solitude* is its air of transparency, of not being a code at all, even a metaphorical one. I shall look a little more closely at the structure of this transparency but first I need to trace a further twist or two in the theme of writing.

The book of Gabriel

Melquíades has a number of delegates and allies in the novel, including various members of the Buendía family and also two other characters who live in his world and manage to migrate from it; the owner of a bookstore in Macondo, and a young man called Gabriel Márquez.

The bookstore is the place where Aureliano Babilonia finds his Sanskrit primer, and it is owned by a wise Catalan, or a Catalan sage, 'un sabio catalán', who arrived in Latin America as a refugee from what the narrator laconically calls 'one of so many wars' [345: 367]. He is a former Classics teacher and an instigator of learning which is both arcane and occasionally functional, like José Arcadio Buendía's curiosity. For the Catalan, 'wisdom was worth nothing if it could not be used to invent a new way of preparing chickpeas' [337: 357]. This is both a pose and a credo. The Catalan, like José Arcadio Buendía, loves useless wisdom but likes to think of wisdom as useful too. When Aureliano Babilonia first meets the Catalan he has two drawers full of scribbled pages 'that in some way made one think of Melquíades' parchments' [345–346: 368]. 'In some way', 'de algun modo' is clumsy, and may be a sign that García Márquez is getting tired – this is the last chapter – but the connection is interesting.

The Catalan, as García Márquez and all his commentators say, is a homage to Ramón Vinyes, a Baranquilla writer who had earlier owned a bookstore, and who was an important focus and influence for García Márquez and his friends in the late 1940s. Vinyes returned to Spain in 1950, and the wise Catalan of the novel, defeated by a nostalgia for the Mediterranean spring, 'derrotado por la nostalgia de una primavera tenaz' [345: 367], also goes home. He takes his (now three) drawers of writings, but abandons 'the piles of books with which he had borne his exile', saying to his friends, 'This crap I leave to you' [347: 369]. His letters from Spain at first are contented but gradually turn into 'pastoral letters of disillusionment', as he becomes bewildered by 'two nostalgias facing each other like two mirrors' – he misses the Macondo where he used to miss Spain – and loses his 'marvellous sense of unreality'. His last advice to his South American friends is that the past is a lie, that memory has no roads of return [348: 370].

The homage is attractive and important but as readers we need to know less how this character got into the novel than what he is doing there. He represents learning and ir-reverence, a sort of diligent frivolity, the writer not as magus but as scholar and joker. The Catalan is right to think the past is often a lie, that the roads of memory are often dead ends. He is wrong to think the story finishes there. Fiction for García Márquez is the replacement of damaged or abolished memory, and therefore can't rest with nostalgia, even if doubled or tripled or multiplied to infinity. The sense of unreality lost at last by the Catalan is presumably just the sense of the world that Melquíades embodies and transcribes and which García Márquez has spent a whole novel trying to make available to us. This is to say that the Catalan is the writer García Márquez might have been but wasn't. It is significant that he should be a European, that the solitude of Latin America is not finally his.

Hanging out in the Catalan's shop when Aureliano Babilonia begins to go there are four friends, all literary-minded, all dedicated to the task of creating work that will last, 'algo perdurable' [339: 359]. The swiftest of dips into biography will tell us that this group is a reconstruction of García Márquez' Baranquilla circle, under their own first names: Álvaro (Cepeda), Germán (Vargas), Alfonso (Fuen-mayor). The fourth friend, Gabriel, is a descendant of Gerineldo Márquez, Colonel Aureliano Buendía's companion-in-arms. These young men are said to be the first and last friends Aureliano Babilonia has [336: 357], but he feels closest to Gabriel because he and Gabriel are the only ones who still believe not only in the deeds of their revolutionary forbears and in the later massacre of the strikers, but in the banana company itself, which has been erased from all legal documents and school texts. Aureliano and Gabriel are thus joined in what is memorably called 'a kind of complicity based on real facts that no one believed in', 'una especie de complicidad fundada en hechos reales en los que nadie creía [338: 359]. We have already seen these unlikely, unbelieved realities, in the account of the massacre itself. The truth is not dead or illusory in such a world, but it is largely inoperative, dependent for its mere continuation on the faith of isolated believers.

For Aureliano there is no escape from this world. It is his world, and he will end with it. But Gabriel wins a trip to Paris as a prize in a French competition, and takes off in a subordinate clause, like Mrs Dalloway dying in a bracket. He travels with 'two changes of clothing, a pair of shoes, and the complete works of Rabelais' [349: 371]. Aureliano imagines him sleeping by day and writing by night in order to stave off hunger, and living in the room where a small child dies in *Rayuela*, a novel by Julio Cortázar [351: 374].

García Márquez says he took with him to Paris not Rabelais but Defoe's *History of the Plague Year*. This rather owlish correction tends to reinforce rather than to diminish the identity. There is a Gabriel Márquez on the cover of this book and in its pages. But it is an identity which is at the service of the fiction, not a miniature confession. García Márquez borrows details from his own life the way he borrows phrases and characters from Juan Rulfo, Carlos Fuentes, Alejo Carpentier, and Cortázar. The suggestion is not that history and fiction are the same, but that the borders take a lot of traffic, and have been known to shift. Gabriel is not the godlike Author, back from the death Roland Barthes consigned him to, and not just a private joke. He is not quite Melquíades' heir either. He is the recreating novelist, our uncertain substitute for the precise prophet. He is a vestige, a removed remnant of Macondo, a possible refiner of nostalgia into lasting work, a man whose inventions may repair a broken memory. He doesn't have to write *this* book – in Paris García Márquez worked on *No One Writes to the Colonel* and *In Evil Hour* – only to represent someone who could write it, who could reach us with news of the vanished Macondo, 'city of mirrors (or mirages)' [360: 383], home and paradigm of real facts delivered to unbelief.

Chapter 5

Invisible ink

'Well, I've often seen a cat without a grin,' thought Alice;
'but a grin without a cat!'   Lewis Carroll

The limits of reality

Situated somewhere between thematic and formal concerns is
the question of how we are to take what is offered to us as
'reality' in *One Hundred Years of Solitude*. When García
Márquez insists that everything in his novel is 'based on reality', he seems in practice to mean two things, although not
always both of them at once. First, that the most fantastic
things have actually been believed or asserted by live people
somewhere, and often in Latin America. This doesn't make
these things true but it may make them real, and they are undoubtedly part of what George Eliot called the scenery of
events, both in and out of novels. The yellow butterflies
which trail after one of his characters were suggested, García
Márquez says, by a remark of his grandmother's about a but-
terfly following a man. Remedios, the beautiful girl who
takes off into the sky and vanishes, is a deadpan rendering of
an excuse García Márquez once heard for a girl who had suddenly left home, probably in some sort of disgrace: she
hadn't run off, it was said, she had ascended into heaven.
He borrows this dizzying excuse as his fictional reality
and then puts the literal truth into his novel as an idle,
misplaced speculation, what foreigners wrongly think must
have happened: 'the family was trying to save its honour
with the wild tale of levitation' [208: 223]. The fantastic thus becomes quite ordinary, what is known by
everyone (principal characters and sympathetic readers)

familiar with this world; and what elsewhere would be plausible becomes merely the lame recourse of ignorance.

Secondly, 'based on reality' means genuinely in touch with some fact of feeling, however hyperbolically or metaphorically expressed. When José Arcadio Buendía dies a rain of tiny yellow flowers falls on Macondo, a 'silent storm' which covers the roofs, carpets the streets and suffocates the animals. This is a miracle even in Macondo – the stuff of legend for the end of a legendary character, the burial of the king, 'el sepelio del rey', as a returning Indian solemnly says [128: 137]. But the miracle affords the truth of a fitting image, the appropriateness of the imagination's rising to the grand occasion, as we feel nature ought to but usually won't.

The rain in Macondo entertains even more elaborate relations with reality. García Márquez had already experimented with the weather as discursive, implied metaphor in his haunting story 'Isabel watching the rain in Macondo', but the rain in *One Hundred Years of Solitude* becomes a major historical catastrophe, a tropical season bloated into disaster. 'It can't rain for ever,' a character says [280: 298], and it can't, even in this book. But it feels as if it can, both in the book and in many places beyond it, and no amount of hyperbole could exaggerate how unending such rain actually seems, how tropical the tropics are. Ruskin thought the pathetic fallacy dealt in just this sort of feeling, and would have regarded García Márquez as a writer of the second order for giving in to it. But Ruskin also saw that there are some subjects which *ought* to throw even a great writer off his balance, points where 'all feverish and wild fancy becomes just true' – not because it *is* true but because metaphor has become inescapable, because we are convinced that there is no other way of coping with the astonishments of the world. García Márquez' mischief is to pretend, but only to pretend, that the pathetic fallacy and its relatives are *always* true.

If we put the two senses of 'based on reality' together, we see that the world of *One Hundred Years of Solitude* is a place where beliefs and metaphors become forms of fact, and where more ordinary facts become uncertain. However, this uncertainty doesn't translate, as critics of García Márquez have been tempted to suggest, into a scepticism about the existence of facts, or into a loose and easy belief that reality just *is* fantastic down Colombia way. The texture of the novel is made up of legends treated as truths — because they are truths to those who believe them — but also (as we have seen) of real facts that no one believes in. The idealist implications of promoting legend to (fictional) fact are countered by the assumption of a firm materialism — the difficulty for this materialism being not to establish the facts but to keep them on the record. The mere truth — say the murder of 3,000 people in one day — is horribly vulnerable to denial and distortion, and the benign family legends of the early pages of the book soon give way to the harsh legends of a corrupt government. When the relatives of the massacred workers and the victims of the subsequent clean-up try to find out what has happened they are told that *nothing* has happened; 'This is a happy town' [270: 287]. We catch the echo of the 'truly happy village, where no one . . . had died' [16: 18], but only to see the contrast. We had no reason to distrust the narrator's earlier words, we have every reason to distrust the new, mealy-mouthed formula. This is not a happy town, and many have died. The reality of these deaths is not in doubt — for the reader, or for the two improbable survivors we looked at in an earlier chapter. What is in doubt is whether these deaths can find a lodging in history, and therefore in what will effectively come to be the past reality of Macondo.

There is a passage in *One Hundred Years of Solitude* which seems to offer its own epistemological theory, or at least to frame the crucial question. The ostensible topic is the speed of change in Macondo, the arrival of the railway, electricity, the cinema, the telephone, the gramophone, while the ghost of José Arcadio Buendía gets increasingly cross in the courtyard of the house:

It was as if God had decided to put to the test every capacity for surprise and was keeping the inhabitants of Macondo in a permanent alternation between excitement and disappointment, doubt and

revelation, to such an extreme that no one knew for certain where
the limits of reality lay.   [198: 212]

The sleight of hand here within the text is similar to that exer-
cised between source and text in the case of the young girl's
ascension to heaven. The old, long-accepted ghost is treated
as obviously real while the new inventions, which are facts for
us, look like crazy illusions in Macondo. It is worth noting
that on at least two occasions García Márquez stealthily
applies the phrase 'in reality' where we might well expect a
quite different phrase, even in the unlikely world of this
novel. 'In reality', the only person the insane (but not yet
ghostly) José Arcadio Buendía could talk to in his latter days,
was . . . Prudencio Aguilar, a ghost [127: 136]; and
Aureliano Babilonia seems to be talking to himself, when 'in
reality' he is having a conversation with the spectral Melquíades [309: 328].

The word *reality* itself does double duty; it mirrors belief
but also buries the question of belief. Reality, in *One Hundred Years of Solitude* as elsewhere, is the realm of common
practice, of what is generally taken to be the case, the
opposite of what is unmasked as illusion or ignorance. 'War'
is only a word for the people left in Macondo until it turns
into a 'dramatic reality' [107: 115]. A 'real basis' for thought
is a sensible political basis, a genuine cause for worry [178:
191]; the 'reality of the nation' is the way things work [176:
189]. An 'accusing halo of reality' surrounds faces which are
finally stripped of affectations [237: 253].

The Macondinos share many of our certainties and our use
of the word *reality* − it's just that their certainties are in-
vaded by unlikely messages and developments. They take
strange things to be the case, and their means of testing reality
are flimsier than ours. Ours are flimsy enough, though;
flimsier than we usually care to think, and one of García
Márquez' discreet polemical aims must be to remind us of
this. Knowing where the limits of reality are may merely mean
knowing how far we want to look. I'm not thinking of anything supernatural or otherworldly, only of other cultures,
and of forms of human behaviour, even within our culture,

which we can't predict and can't imagine, even when we are assured of their truth. Some murders, for example; many pathologies. Or the appearance of a pig's tail on a human child. This, we might feel, can safely be ascribed to the realm of fiction, somewhere even beyond hyperbole. But in 1988 the *British Medical Journal* reported just such a case not in Macondo but in Manchester. The surgeon who operated on the child to remove the addendum said, 'It was a true tail, an extension of the coccyx, moved intermittently and was covered with fine downy hair.' Unlike his counterpart in *One Hundred Years of Solitude*, the child suffered no ill effects, and when last heard of was a healthy five-year-old.

Tone

The chief vehicle for García Márquez' vision of reality's astonishments is his unastonished tone, his refusal of the questions or comments which the state of his (and our) culture would seem to require. Flying carpets? Ghosts? Miracles? The writer of fantastic literature, in Todorov's terms, would have to say how fantastic these things were; the writer of tales of the marvellous would express no surprise but would have to place these phenomena in a secondary, specially developed world. Todorov's word for what happens in García Márquez is the *fabulous* — the supernatural 'exists in so far as people believe in it'. This line of thought clears up some puzzles, as I have suggested; and starts a few more. Does the author/narrator believe in his fables as he tells them? The question seems to me haunting and inevitable but also quite unanswerable, the precise result of a style, rather like Flaubert's famed disappearance into his text. 'The author in his work', Flaubert said in a letter to Louise Colet [9 December 1852], 'must be like God in the universe, present everywhere and visible nowhere. The effect, for the spectator, must be a kind of amazement. How has that been done? he should say, and he should feel crushed without knowing why.' García Márquez doesn't want to crush us, but he does want us to think for ourselves about the limits of reality.

The tone of *One Hundred Years of Solitude* works as a strongly felt silence or absence, a smile which fades before it starts, like an improvement on the Cheshire cat, a grin without even a grin. We can't say the narrator is simply ironic, a disbeliever in his story, because there are no signs that he is. Yet we can't make him a *naif*, a mere echo of his characters' erratic sense of the world. I have used the word *deadpan* several times in this book, and I think that gets quite close to the effect, a sort of linguistic face of Buster Keaton. But we have to remember that the deadpan strictly tells us *nothing*, not even that it is not as serious as it looks. What it does do is court our suspicion, so that we feel that whatever it is up to it is not saying just what it says or only what it says. It is a form of irony, but so faint on the surface that irony seems too assertive a word for it.

García Márquez took a long time finding this tone, couldn't write this novel without it, and hasn't, I think, quite managed it anywhere else in his work — it slips very easily into whimsy or mock innocence. It involves a carefully pitched appearance of credulity, and he adapted it, he says, from the examples of his grandmother and Franz Kafka. There is a touch of the deadpan about this assertion too, but we can risk taking it seriously if we don't take it mechanically. García Márquez makes the connection twice in his conversations with his friend Apuleyo Mendoza. 'My grandmother . . . used to tell me about the most atrocious things without turning a hair, as if it was something she'd just seen. I realized that it was her impassive manner and her wealth of images that made her stories so credible. I wrote *One Hundred Years of Solitude* using my grandmother's method.' We should add that the borrowing can't be as simple as he makes it sound; that the method encompasses not only atrocious but also lovely and impossible things; and that being credible can't really be its chief goal. It allows the historical and the fabulous to lie side by side without quarrelling, and it asks, not for belief or even a suspension of disbelief, but for something like a suspension of surprise. 'Kafka', García Márquez continues, 'recounted things the same way my grandmother used to. When I read *Metamorphosis*, at seventeen, I realized I could be a writer.' And again: 'I remember the first sentence, "As Gregor Samsa awoke one morning from uneasy dreams he found himself transformed in his bed into a gigantic insect." "Bloody hell!" I thought, "my grandmother used to talk like that." ' Gregor Samsa is in fact in even more trouble than García Márquez' Spanish memory suggests, since he is changed not into a single insect but into an odd plural, a vermin, an *Ungeziefer*, the grammatical impossibility compounding the impossible biology. What is striking about Kafka's sentence, of course, is its calm, its extraordinary refusal to be ruffled, and this is the effect García Márquez strives for (and gets) in *One Hundred Years of Solitude*. Of course the grandmother's and Kafka's interests and moods are different, and García Márquez' are different again. The grandmother presumably took the atrocious things she told to be normal, and therefore really didn't turn a hair; for her the method was not a method. Kafka affects to treat the desperate and the monstrous as if it were the everyday, as if language could proceed untouched by what it reports, and the very modesty of the voice enhances the nightmare. García Márquez needs his tone to build up an unreliable but unquestioned world, a place irremediably soaked in myth, where legend, hyperbole, metaphor, and fact all arrive in the mind as *stories*, coloured in all kinds of ways by need and innocence and expectation. His trick is to refuse to discriminate among the stories, to relate them all as features of *what is*. This is the world of the grandmother discreetly complicated by the intelligence of the invisible grin; the world of Kafka rendered (largely) more benign but also more extensive. There is quite a bit of anger in this novel, I think, an anger at the very doom which provides the plot, at the imprisonment in myth which the novel has taken as its fictional and historical field. But the anger isn't paraded, doesn't gesticulate, and of course many of the imprisoning myths have enormous charm anyway. They allow one to stay human in the prison, but then the charm is also one of the prison's most terrible strengths.

For an extended example of the tone at work we may look
at the account of the death of Amaranta, Colonel Aureliano
Buendía's sister. First a figure of speech is taken literally,
with no signal of change of gear or level. Amaranta is not
worried about when she will die because she already knows:
'Death had awarded her the privilege of announcing itself
several years ahead of time' [243: 259]. The almost invisible
personification (death awarding a privilege) turns immedi-
ately, in the next sentence, into a new character. Death is 'a
woman dressed in blue with long hair, with a sort of anti-
quated look . . . On one occasion she asked Amaranta to
thread her needle for her' [243: 259–260]. Next a rather interesting superstition is treated as if it were the most ordinary
of assumptions. Amaranta thinks it will be a kindness, and
perhaps a reparation for some of her harshnesses, if she takes
with her when she dies any letters the townspeople may wish
to send to the dead. 'The news that Amaranta Buendía was
sailing at dusk carrying the mail of death spread throughout
Macondo before noon, and at three in the afternoon there
was a whole box full of letters in the parlor' [244: 261]. The
scene 'seemed a complete farce', the narrator says, but not
because of the letters. What seems farcical is that Amaranta
doesn't look ill at all, *isn't* ill, and therefore can hardly be
dying. She shares out her worldly goods among the poor,
refuses a last confession. 'Lying on cushions, as if she really
were ill, she braided her long hair and rolled it about her ears
as death had told her it should be . . .' She looks at a mirror,
talks to her mother; and her actual dying is then reported
simply as 'the news' another character, away from the house,
receives [246: 262–263].

The mode of writing here is a particularly straight-faced
variety of indirect free style. It doesn't do much miming of
the voices of the character or the community, but it strictly
(if tacitly) adopts their point of view. No visible irony or scepticism plays in the prose, except possibly in the irreverent *was
sailing, zarpaba*, as if Amaranta were a sailboat, or a new
Columbus. A more rationalistic narrative would have insisted
on the subjectivity of these perceptions – Amaranta thought

she saw Death, the townspeople imagined letters could be taken to the afterlife — but here they are offered to us as entirely accurate and plausible, indeed the inability to share them is implicitly viewed as slightly strange. Another character can't see Death when Amaranta does ' in spite of the fact that she was so real, so human' [243: 260]. What would have caused doubt even in a ghost story — only the protagonist sees the creature — here seems merely an odd blindness in others.

There are elements in the story of Amaranta's end which are frankly fantastic, and seen as such by narrator and characters; but the tone, while registering epistemological difference, still shows very little surprise and won't adjudicate. In another context we might want to think of Amaranta as willing her death, and I'm not sure this notion is not faintly present in some submerged fashion, since Amaranta's ferocious and unrelenting will is so much part of her character. But her will did not permit her to outlive Rebeca, as she longed to, and mainly we are asked here simply to assent to the extraordinary. Gregor Samsa became vermin and Amaranta Buendía got her death-day right, and died without illness. That is the story, these are strange doings, but there is no riddle.

Our assent involves a double inference or agreement, I think: that a world of the imagination has licences and possibilities which the material world does not; and that the material world itself is a very strange place, so that only something like this casual-seeming investment in strangeness can give us the feel of it. Úrsula has no doubt that her daughter has genuine foreknowledge of her death, and she is undisturbed by the signs of health, because she knows that 'the Buendías died without illness' [245: 261]. But she is worried lest the eager correspondents of Macondo, anxious to see their postlady on her way, should bury Amaranta alive. This splendid display of practical concern amid a mild acceptance of the most baroque assumptions offers a tiny instance of the effect the whole novel is after. It is rather as if we were to fuss at the documentary details of a miracle — the miracle is implicitly welcomed but at the same time a certain scandal or

extravagance in it is underlined. There is a gag of just this
kind in the story of the priest who uses a display of levitation
as an unorthodox mode of fund-raising. He resorts to this
device, we are told, because he is 'confused by his despera-
tion' over the irreligiousness of the Macondinos. He takes a
sip of hot chocolate, wipes his mouth, spreads his arms and
closes his eyes. Then he lifts some twelve centimetres off the
ground. This is, he claims 'an undeniable proof of the infinite
power of God' [79: 85]. Most of the townspeople are im-
pressed, but not José Arcadio Buendía, and not the narrator. There is no sense that the levitation proves anything at
all; no sense either that it doesn't actually take place. It's just
another Macondo mystery, like a precisely announced or a
perfectly unexplained death.

Diction

What I have been calling tone is a relation of narrator to nar-
rated material, an unperturbed reporting of whatever comes
up. I'd like to look now at the diction of *One Hundred Years
of Solitude* — we can think of diction as reflecting the
author's relation to his narrator through the language he
allows him. García Márquez' performance is less assured
here, or at least takes some time to settle down. The difficulty
seems to lie in the recalcitrant, old-fashioned fine writing
which won't at first go away. It is full of important,
ambitious adjectives, as if to imitate Conrad on a spree. We
read of an 'immense desolation' [27: 30], an 'irremediable
nostalgia' [30: 34], of the 'implacable time-keeping of the
lapwings', 'el horario implacable de los alcaravanes' [104:
112]. There are lots of fondly balanced phrases; 'She knew
. . . the haughtiness of her spirit, and she was frightened by
the virulence of her anger' [72: 78]; 'He felt the ridges of
veins, the pulse of misfortune' [105: 112]. There are plenty
of Flaubertian lists:

He got dressed . . . listening in the dark to his brother's calm
breathing, the dry cough of his father in the next room, the asthma
of the hens in the courtyard, the buzz of the mosquitoes, the beating

of his heart and the inordinate bustle of a world that he had not
noticed until then . . .   [30: 33–34]

At times we get both balances and lists: 'She had lost the
strength of her thighs, the firmness of her breasts, the habit
of her tenderness, but she preserved intact the madness of her
heart . . .' [31: 35]; 'he felt . . . the security of power . . .
knew the uncertainty of love . . . found ridiculous the for-
mality of death' [110: 118]. We are a long way from
Nabokov's reckless literary fun with such formulas in *Lolita*.

The trouble with such writing is its self-admiration and its
solemnity. It can be elegant, of course, but it has the elegance
of a procession. Borges writes like this when he is nodding,
or running out of irony, and a whole conservative Latin
American culture writes like it all the time. The effect is not
as fussy in Spanish as it would be in English, but it is predict-
able, and we need to notice it if we are to see what García
Márquez finally does with this unpromising idiom, what a
marvellous instrument he makes of it once he gets going.

The language begins more and more to wear invisible
quotation marks, to go out of its way to court cliché,
although it usually stops short of outright parody. We
read, for example, of the 'inclement destiny' of one Roque
Carnicero. We know the cliché is deliberate, a slightly too
high-flown flourish, because of the contrast with the way
Roque himself sees his fate: 'There's no getting away from
bad luck. I was born a son of a bitch and I'm going to die a
son of a bitch' [117: 125]. Or the idiom lifts into an exaggeration of its own fine manner and we hear of Aureliano
Segundo's 'modest tourneys of voracity' [293: 311], and of
Amaranta's dragging with her toward death a 'fragrant and
worm-eaten guava grove of love', a 'fragante y agusanado
guayabal de amor' [242: 258] – all the stored and spoiled
passion she has not spent, wittily and casually pictured in ripe
and too tropical prose. Death itself is courteously seen as put-
ting oneself 'at the disposition of the worms' [242: 259] –
the politeness both acknowledges and heads off a grisly fear.

Diction joins tone here. The author vanishes behind his
amused narrator, who vanishes into his grin. Gerineldo

Márquez, companion-in-arms of Colonel Aureliano Buendía
and former suitor to Amaranta, maintains contact with the
rebel officers even after the Peace of Neerlandia has been
signed:

> With them he waged the sad war of daily humiliation, of entreaties
> and petitions, of come-back-tomorrow, of any-time-now, of we're-
> studying-your-case-with-the-proper-attention; the war hopelessly
> lost against the many yours-most-trulys who should have signed and
> would never sign the lifetime pensions. The other war, the bloody
> one of twenty years, did not cause them as much damage as the cor-
> rosive war of eternal postponements. Even Colonel Gerineldo Már-
> quez, who escaped three attempts on his life, survived five wounds,
> and emerged unscathed from innumerable battles, succumbed to
> that atrocious siege of waiting and sank into the miserable defeat of
> old age, thinking of Amaranta among the diamond-shaped patches
> of light in a borrowed house.   [213–214: 228]

Only 'the miserable defeat of old age' is at all weak here, a
touch too sentimental. 'The atrocious siege of waiting'
doesn't quite catch the right meaning for 'el asedio atroz de
la espera' but I can't do better. The suggestion is not that the
man waits out a siege but that he is besieged *by* waiting, that
what is atrocious is the interminable patience of this new, intangible enemy. The 'sad war' and the 'daily humiliation' are
flat and exact, and the voices of officialdom are expertly
mimicked. The borrowed house and the diamond-shaped
light serve to remind us that we are in the minutely imagined
world of a novelist. The house adds pathos and speaks of
money (or the lack of it); the light allows us to visualize the
man, to perceive his sunken condition as a picture, that of the
shabby, memory-struck Harlequin.

Narrative movement

The story line of *One Hundred Years of Solitude* proceeds at
first (and at the beginning of the second half of the book) by
a sequence of loops and flashbacks, but more generally settles
into a system of rather unnerving alternations, governed, it
seems, by an active principle of narrative interruption. There
are plenty of cycles and repetitions in the novel, but

more striking still is this sense of parallel but broken tracks – our attention brusquely switched from one to the other and back, as if to test and find wanting our ability to hold enough stories in our minds at once.

The loops and flashbacks can be quickly described, although even they are not as complete or circular as they may seem. The ice mentioned in the novel's first sentence appears in the last paragraphs of the first chapter, closing a long parenthesis which has included: the gypsies' visits and inventions, Melquíades and his reported death, the design and building of Macondo, José Arcadio Buendía's dabblings in alchemy and astronomy, his excursions in quest of civilization, the education of the two boys. The next chapter takes us further back into the past, giving us the prehistory of the present family (Francis Drake attacks Riohacha), the story of José Arcadio Buendía's quarrel with Prudencio Aguilar, and more details of the founding of Macondo. This second, further-reaching flashback closes with José Arcadio Buendía's dream of the city of mirrors:

José Arcadio Buendía dreamed that night that right there a noisy city with houses having mirror walls rose up. He asked what city it was and they answered him with a name that he had never heard, that had no meaning at all, but that had a supernatural echo in his dream: Macondo. On the following day he convinced his men that they would never find the sea. He ordered them to cut down trees to make a clearing beside the river, at the coolest spot on the bank, and there they founded the village.   [28: 31–32]

We have been waiting for the ice to return, to do something to deserve its promised narrative prominence, and José Arcadio Buendía seems to tie up the symbolic order for us. The mirror walls were a prediction of the ice, he decides in retrospect, they looked forward to the new wintry Macondo, the frozen tropic which the invention of ice would make possible. Except that it wouldn't. The ice was just ice, you couldn't build a city of it, and the mirrors were not a prediction. Or they were a prediction only of an ultimate unreality, as the last page of the novel suggests. Mirrors offer reversed and two-dimensional effigies of people, who don't bleed or fall when you shoot them but just fragment, turn into shards, like the images of Rita Hayworth in the funfair in Orson Welles' *Lady from Shanghai*; and a sort of linguistic slither converts the city of mirrors into a city of mirages: 'la ciudad de los espejos (o los espejismos)' [360: 383]. The ice *is* a figure for a certain coldness in the family, and especially in Colonel Aureliano Buendía, and we can see it as earning its narrative keep in this way if we wish. But mainly it functions as a broken or only half-kept promise, something that seemed as if it would mean more than it did. It hangs in Aureliano's memory because it is one of the wonders of his childhood, a synecdoche for a whole vanished world, and it hangs in our memory because it is a fine image of what a world of heat doesn't know. But the ice has no story; leads to no story. It just looks as if it might.

The second half of the novel begins as we have seen with another promise ('Years later on his deathbed Aureliano Segundo was to remember . . .'), and also with a splendid jumbling of narrative orders, as if the writer had tried for Melquíades' effect of simultaneity and instead got everything backwards. We hear of Aureliano Segundo's memory of his child before we hear of his own childhood; and of the child before we hear of the mother. We learn of Aureliano Segundo's lifelong passion for his mistress before we learn anything about his lengthy marriage. We meet Fernanda, his wife, on the first page of the tenth chapter, but get the details of her arrival in Macondo as carnival queen on the last pages; and get the details of Aureliano Segundo's earlier search for her only in the chapter after that.

The very frequency of flashbacks in novels is being spoofed here, I think, as a writer's tic or habit, and there is also a suggestion of time in a hurry, of a future in Macondo which can't wait for the present to pass, a galloping toward what looks like an end. García Márquez is spoofing this haste because it is so much a temptation of all story-telling – the trick is not to have a good ending, but to stave it off in interesting ways – and because his own vision involves a persistent worry about endings, with all the settled, pacified meanings they seem to propose.

In this sense the flashbacks themselves point us toward the central narrative strategy of *One Hundred Years of Solitude*, toward what I have called the principle of interruption. The broken promise of the ice is a small version of many broken promises. I don't mean that stories don't end in this novel. They often end amusingly and well; or beautifully and darkly. The whole history of the family completes a prophecy. I mean stories are so often broken into, dislocated, delayed, forgotten, that we don't know where to expect them, and some of them turn out not to be stories at all. The effect is rather like that created by those children's jokes which have no point, no punch-line. We laugh not because our expectations have been cheated or diverted, but because the very notion of expectation has momentarily been ruined. García Márquez is too kind, too much the dedicated story-teller, to ruin expectation, but he does keep setting traps for our craving for finality; leaves us with mysteries, or with coherences which mock our appetite for coherence. A destiny is a story, I have suggested. But a story is also a destiny, and we need to be wary of it for the same reasons.

Some stories seem to end too soon. The Colonel goes off to war, and instead of the rousing chronological account we may want, we get a dead, bare list — the equivalent of telling someone the end of a movie they have just started watching:

Colonel Aureliano Buendía organized thirty-two armed uprisings and he lost them all. He had seventeen male children by seventeen different women and they were exterminated one after the other on a single night before the oldest one had reached the age of thirty-five. He survived fourteen attempts on his life, seventy-three ambushes, and a firing squad. He lived through a dose of strychnine in his coffee that was enough to kill a horse. He refused the Order of Merit, which the President of the Republic awarded him. He rose to be Commander in Chief of the revolutionary forces, with jurisdiction and command from one border to another, and the man most feared by the government, but he never let himself be photographed. He declined the lifetime pension offered him after the war and until old age he made his living from the little gold fishes that he manufactured in his workshop in Macondo. Although he always fought at the head of his men, the only wound that he received was the one he gave himself after signing the Treaty of Neerlandia, which put an end to almost twenty years of civil war. He shot himself in the chest with a pistol and the bullet came out through his back without damaging any vital organ. The only thing left of all that was a street that bore his name in Macondo.   [97: 104]

Of course the deadness of the list has its daunting power – the numbers alone are hair-raising. Nevertheless, the principal effect here is the destruction of suspense, a narrative incontinence. It is a fuller version of the firing squad which pounces into the very first sentence of the book. We wonder what can be left to tell. Well, nearly everything is left to tell, but that is what we have slowly to learn, against the odds, against the feeling of having arrived before we have properly set out.

Most of the stories in *One Hundred Years of Solitude* end, however, if they end at all, only after suffering interruptions from other stories. The method is not unlike that of the digression in *Tristram Shandy*, except that García Márquez is aiming for a regularity of effect quite alien to Sterne, a genuine alternation, something like a set of sudden and repeated changes of musical key. He seems to have discovered the full range of possibilities of this device in his astonishing fifth chapter, which is well worth a closer look.

In this chapter the withdrawn, apolitical Aureliano becomes a revolutionary. 'This is madness, Aurelito', his father-in-law says right at the end of the chapter as Aureliano sets off to join the rebel forces. 'Not madness at all', Aureliano replies. 'It's war. And don't call me Aurelito again, because I am Colonel Aureliano Buendía' [96: 103]. In other words, this chapter concerns the invasion of politics into Macondo and private life, yet it reads as if this invasion were not its topic but a strange surprise, something the narrator has recently stumbled on. The movement is the opposite of remembering the future, and both perspectives are important in the novel. The narrator eagerly remembers and oddly forgets.

The chapter begins 'Aureliano Buendía and Remedios Moscote were married one Sunday in March . . .' [77: 83], seeming to situate us quite firmly in a world of peace and romance. Remedios is very young, and after the ceremony her sisters unthinkingly pick her up to kiss her. However, she is a person of great grace and gaiety, and becomes a much-loved member of the family. Aureliano discovers in her the reason he lacked for living, 'la justificación que le hacía falta para vivir' [83: 90]. When his nephew Arcadio faces the firing squad a few years later, she is the person he thinks of. We soon leave the marriage for other stories: that of the arrival of the priest and his 'levitation by means of chocolate' [79: 86], the discovery that the words the insane José Arcadio Buendía is barking are Latin; above all the story of Rebeca's much-postponed wedding and Amaranta's fervid jealousy of her. This wedding is finally about to take place when 'a major obstacle' falls in its way: the sudden death of little Remedios in pregnancy [83: 89]. The girl, who seemed to be living her own happy story, is a grim event in someone else's, a complication, a narrative deferment. The shock is all the greater because, as I said earlier, the language of *was to* seemed to promise Remedios a much longer life: another destiny unravelled. It seems heartless of the narrator to call her an obstacle, but that is one of the tougher effects of the imperturbable tone, and here as elsewhere we do tend to supply the emotions he will not name or evoke.

One story is interrupted by an inconsolable twist in another, an imitation of arbitrariness which may leave us sharing Aureliano's rage at what would be an injustice if it were not meaningless. Later in the chapter, when Rebeca has been swept off her feet by the massive José Arcadio, back from his flight with the gypsies, Rebeca's fiancé Pietro Crespi becomes Amaranta's suitor, but then *their* marriage is delayed too, because Aureliano abruptly says, 'This is no time to go around thinking about weddings' [90: 97]. Why not? Because the civil war is almost upon them, and this is how we hear about it. The implication, I take it, is not that war is as arbitrary as Remedios' death, but that that is how it will feel until you understand it: just another harsh, unmotivated incursion, an affliction like a plague.

That is how all stories feel when we are only characters in them.

The system of alternation is everywhere. Macondo's carnival turns into a massacre because it is abruptly caught up in Aureliano's old story – the sadness being that he has no story, at least no political story, at that point. The amazing tale of Remedios the Beauty's ascension to heaven would have kept Macondo talking for some time, we are told, 'if the barbarous extermination of the Aurelianos [i.e. sixteen of Aureliano's seventeen war-born sons] had not replaced amazement with horror' [208–209: 223 – the English text here has 'honor', which must be a misprint]. Fernanda takes her erring daughter Meme into exile and returns on a train 'protected by armed police' [258: 275], a cue for the story of the political tension in Macondo and the coming strike. The cue is scarcely acknowledged though, and the narrative returns to Meme's story, with a nun bringing her child Aureliano to Macondo. After that the political trouble breaks out 'without any warning' [260: 278], the narrator says, not entirely truthfully, but giving us a nice hint as to how the system works.

There is a particularly beautiful example of the system at work in a later chapter where Fernanda's management of the house is being described. The rain seems to be everywhere, but Fernanda doesn't change her strict routine. No one even looks out of doors any more, and this is fine with the pious Fernanda, because she thinks doors are made to be closed, and that curiosity about life on the street is 'a matter for harlots'. 'Nevertheless', we are told, 'she was the first to look out when. . .' And with this the topic switches: what Fernanda sees in the street has nothing at all to do with her housekeeping, since it is the sodden funeral procession of Gerineldo Márquez, an extraordinary image of Aureliano's world in drowned defeat:

A more desolate cortege could not have been imagined. They had put the coffin in an oxcart over which they built a canopy of banana leaves, but the pressure of the rain was so intense and the streets so muddy that with every step the wheels got stuck . . . Behind the cart, some barefoot and all of them with their pants rolled up, splashing in the mud were the last survivors of the surrender at Neerlandia . . . They appeared like an unreal vision along the street which still bore the name of Colonel Aureliano Buendía . . .   [278: 295]

This procession, like the strike, like the murder of the Aurelianos, like the carnival massacre, like the civil war, like the death of little Remedios, arrives not only unannounced but on the wings of a quite different story.

For a comparable use of this narrative principle we may glance at the reckless story line of Luis Buñuel's film *The Phantom of Liberty* 1974. A man has a bad dream and goes to see his doctor. While he is in the surgery, the doctor's nurse interrupts to ask if she can have some tíme off to visit her ailing father, and the story now follows her, abandoning the first man, never to return. The nurse gives a lift to a man about to lecture to a police academy, and the story, forgetting the nurse, pursues him to his lecture. And so on, through several more relays and losses of what looked like a point. But Buñuel's and García Márquez' interests are in the end quite different. For Buñuel the narrative sprawl is an attack on relevance and meaning, or rather on the terrible confidence with which we take those things for granted. The stories could go anywhere, other stories could be picked up and dropped, the implied movement is toward secession, dispersion. For García Márquez the stories all belong together, can't get out of each other's way. No story is an island, entire of itself, and the only escape from stories is into other stories. This is one of the reasons why *One Hundred Years of Solitude* offers so strong a sense of a world.

But it is a world which doesn't know it is one, and stories in it fall upon one another as if in an ambush. There is always a story behind you, but you are always startled by it. Sometimes the stories appear as quick shadows, prophecies plucked from the future, as we have seen, but also echoes from the past. The 'enchanted region' of the opening chapter [18: 20] becomes a banana plantation [202: 216]; late in the novel the once seemingly lost sea can be seen from the same place [287–288: 305]. The shadows seem to offer a message, perhaps in code, but vanish before we can decipher it. And quite often, of course, not even the shadows are seen by the characters. The Flaubertian list is used to brilliant, flexible effect in the account of all the formerly lively and observant Meme Buendía does *not* see when she is taken away from home:

She did not see the shady, endless banana groves on both sides of the tracks. She did not see the white houses of the gringoes or their gardens, dried out by dust and heat, or the women in shorts and blue-striped shirts playing cards on the terraces. She did not see the oxcarts on the dusty roads loaded down with bunches of bananas. She did not see the girls jumping like fish in the transparent rivers, leaving the passengers on the train with the bitter memory of their splendid breasts; or the motley and miserable shacks of the workers where Mauricio Babilonia's butterflies fluttered, and where green and squalid children sat on their pots in the doorways, and pregnant women shouted insults at the train as it passed . . . She did not look out of the window even when the hot humidity of the plantations ended, and the train crossed the plain of poppies where the charred skeleton of the Spanish galleon still was, and reached the same clear air and the same dirty, foaming sea where the hopes of José Arcadio Buendía had ended almost a century before.

[256: 273–274]

What Meme doesn't see (what we unforgettably do see) is the history of Macondo, written into the landscape and tied to the landmarks of this text: plantations, Americans, galleon, the near and distant ocean. Of course what she doesn't see is also a metaphor, a correlative for what she feels, the tumult behind her silence, a whole world of beauty, exploitation, vitality, death. Still, she stands here for many characters in *One Hundred Years of Solitude*: blind to all that the readers know, removed from any help Melquíades or Gabriel Márquez might wish to offer, the permanent victim of an interruption.

Chapter 5

Love and Death

> 'These casual exfoliations are
> Of the tropic of resemblances. . .'
>
> Wallace Stevens

Shall we dance?

García Márquez felt that *One Hundred Years of Solitude* was
a literary risk of a particular kind. 'Listen to this', he told his
friend Plinio Apuleyo Mendoza. 'When a character in the
book shoots himself, his blood trickles in a thin stream all
round the town until it finds the dead man's mother. The
whole book is like that, on a knife's edge between the sublime
and the vulgar. Like the bolero.' We may note incidentally
that with 'shoots himself' García Márquez seems to solve the
mystery the novel so fastidiously leaves unsolved. But he is
only the author.

A bolero is a Latin American dance tune, smoother and
softer than a rhumba. The lyric typically concerns loneliness
and unhappy love, destiny and ill luck; asks time to stop,
talks to stars and nightingales; says you will always be in my
heart. The form 'may seem excessively sentimental', Apuleyo
Mendoza says, 'but it is also tongue-in-cheek'. The form *is*
sentimental, but that is its virtue. What García Márquez
wanted was the hyperbolic licence of the popular song, and
in this sense the extravagance of the bolero is the exact com-
plement of his deadpan tone. The wildest songs are the ones
you have to sing straight. For an analogy we may think of the
lurid gothic fables that crop up in country and western music
– hearts, for example, left in jars by the door – and indeed
in many straightforward ballads.

76

There are energies in bad taste and sentimentality, or rather in letting go a little of our decorum and our scorn for feeling. There was an arid strain in Modernism — remember the prim Stephen Dedalus, and the tight, frightened inhabitants of Eliot's poems — and it has taken writers some time to reclaim the heart, to recognize that the realms of open feeling should not be left entirely to the songwriters. This is not a 'camp' enjoyment of vulnerability and artlessness, and the tongue doesn't even need to flicker toward the cheek. The argument merely respects the likeable, ungainly truth of popular lyrics, which is kin to that of clichés and old jokes. The songs are not 'authentic', as folk material may be, they are soaked in commercialism, compromised in every possible way. But they are all many people have for the expression of major emotions. They are like Emma Bovary's language to her lover Rodolphe, platitudinous but possibly, in her case, deeply felt; like the affectionate parodies in Proust; like the touching, film-ridden universe of the fiction of Manuel Puig.

García Márquez' later short novel, *Chronicle of a Death Foretold*, is as he says 'the false story of a true crime'; and also the story of that story, a reconstruction of 'the broken mirror of memory'. The crime is a murder, some twenty-seven-years old now, in a Latin American river town. The bolero touch lies in a heightening of the textual effect I have identified in *One Hundred Years of Solitude*, an evocation of necessity and accident in a single thought, wittily articulated in the phrase 'fatal coincidences', 'coincidencias funestas'. The murder seems both inevitable (because it has happened) and quite fortuitous (because it so obviously could have been prevented, because even the murderers, we are told, wanted it to be prevented). A judge examining the case is disturbed by the slither of the story towards popular romance, and feels it cannot be 'legitimate that life should use so many accidents forbidden to literature'; the accidents being everything that in everyday probability would have saved a man's life but in this instance didn't.

García Márquez has worked most deliberately in the bolero line — a touch too deliberately, perhaps — in his recent novel

Love in the Time of Cholera, which is the patient story of a love like a song, a love which literally lasts a lifetime, told almost in the manner of an old-fashioned serial, the *roman-feuilleton*. By 'almost' I mean to suggest that the novel is not an old-fashioned serial but that it isn't far enough away for irony. Even the notion of the deadpan won't apply here. The narrative voice is sober, austere, intelligent, but appears to share all the assumptions of the characters. It is as if *One Hundred Years of Solitude* were written, not by Melquíades or Gabriel but, say, by Amaranta or Pietro Crespi. 'It is a novel', Stephen Minta says of *Love in the Time of Cholera*, 'which constantly challenges the reader to adopt a knowing, cynical, or sophisticated response to the events described, and then works hard to ensure victory for a certain kind of innocence.' The matter could not be better put, but does innocence actually win? The characters are stereotypes, Minta continues, 'capable of revealing the complex truths which all stereotypes more or less successfully conceal'. It's the revelation I'm not sure about. The well-meaning writer is in a quandary here. If he moves away from his stereotypes, he begins to condescend to them, and to drop their truths for his. If he repeats them, he can only gesture vaguely, as they do, toward those complex truths – can hint that they are there, but not focus them with any precision. García Márquez takes the second option, and certainly the book is very engaging, and a bold venture for a writer with a big reputation to wreck; but it may be slightly too much the lowbrow antithesis to the brilliantly literary *Autumn of the Patriarch*, where every device in the Modernist lexicon – interior monologue, parody, multiple narrators, sliding point of view and the rest – was deployed in what is manifestly a work of high art, a contribution to the school of Faulkner and Joyce. García Márquez thinks of that book as 'a much more important literary achievement' than *One Hundred Years of Solitude*, and perhaps it is. But then 'literary' in such a claim would have a slightly restrictive sense, and we might want to say that major works of literature are often less perfectly literary than this – and something more than literary too. *One*

Hundred Years of Solitude neither repeats nor undermines nor avoids stereotypes but sympathetically plays with them, illuminates them; takes them seriously but not submissively. It *is* a literary achievement, one of the century's most visible landmarks, but it is also like a bolero.

The bolero is everywhere in *One Hundred Years of Solitude*, inviting us to sing along, but also plunging us into great gulfs of gloom. 'The house was filled with love', we read in the fourth chapter [64: 69]. This is exactly the love we find in romantic lyrics, frustrated, desperate, a form of desolation, as the text has it [65: 70]; a plague as José Arcadio Buendía calls it [67: 72], anticipating his maker's later writing. The girls Rebeca and Amaranta, as we have seen, are both yearningly in love with Pietro Crespi, the blonde and beautifully dressed pianola expert. Aureliano is hopelessly in love with the child Remedios. He writes poems without beginnings or endings on bits of parchment which Melquíades gives him, on the bathroom walls, on the skin of his own arms.

However, this romantic misery has an end, or looks as if it might. Rebeca's love is reciprocated, she and Pietro are engaged. Aureliano marries Remedios, who, as we noted, charms the whole Buendía family. It is true that Amaranta is left out, and swears that Rebeca's marriage will take place only over her dead body. Or *a* dead body, since she begins to feel she is going to have to put laudanum in Rebeca's coffee just before the wedding. At this point we get the cruel narrative swerve we have already looked at. The undesired death of Remedios provides the desired obstacle. 'Amaranta . . . had begged God with such fervor for something fearful to happen so that she would not have to poison Rebeca that she felt guilty of Remedios' death' [83: 89]. The text later discreetly mentions the 'unintentional laudanum', the 'láudano involuntario' [84: 91], which Amaranta gave Remedios, a wonderful image of the terror and magic of passionate wishing or praying.

Rebeca's engagement to Crespi ends when she is swept away by the returning José Arcadio, marries him and lives tumultuously ever after, until he either does or does not shoot himself one September morning. She then lives on in solitude to become an ancient, forgotten lady in an unvisited house. In context, though, this is not an unhappy love song. Rebeca, as Úrsula understands in her final audit of her family's emotions, was possessed of an 'impatient heart', which had the valour of its impatience and regretted nothing. Rebeca, who is not a Buendía but only takes the name (twice: because she is adopted and because she marries José Arcadio), 'was the only one who had the unbridled courage that Úrsula had wanted for her line' [219: 234].

This is to say that the Buendías are afraid of the heart, however brave they may be against other enemies – although their fear is complicated, a form of vanquished or displaced heroism. The story of Amaranta is exemplary in this sense. With Rebeca out of the way the path is clear for her to marry Crespi, whom she loves. She accepts his courtly attentions, seems to be happy, but then suddenly tells him, with brilliant and startling candour, that the marriage is off, has never really been on: 'Don't be simple, Crespi. I wouldn't marry you even if I were dead' [102: 109]. She is smiling when she says this – a smile which resembles her brother's, and into which much pain and an odd kindness crowd like muted stowaways. Crespi tries every amorous recourse known to him, including an angelic serenade sung in 'a voice that led one to believe that no other person on earth could feel such love' [102: 110], and on the Day of the Dead, all persuasions having failed, cuts his wrists and dies.

We are looking, in Amaranta, at what we may call a vocation for solitude, and at love as a means of inviting and enhancing this vocation, setting its exorbitant price. The vocation is founded on guilt perhaps, rather as Macondo itself is founded on José Arcadio Buendía's having killed a man. Amaranta can't accept a future built on Remedios' magical death – and Crespi's suicide compounds her remorse. She burns her hand in the hearth as a penance, and wears a black bandage for the rest of her life. Úrsula's later thoughts on her daughter are interesting, though. She believes that the bitter Amaranta is the 'most tender woman who had ever existed', and that her behaviour with Crespi reflected not 'a desire for vengeance' but 'a mortal struggle between a measureless love and an invincible cowardice'; that 'the irrational fear Amaranta had always had of her tormented heart had triumphed in the end' [218–219: 233–234]. 'Irrational fear' seems a little casual – with a heart like Amaranta's fear seems entirely rational – but there is an important insight in the picture of love and the terror of love fighting it out, making Amaranta some kind of Latin American cousin of the Princess of Cleves, or any of the world's great, frightened renouncers. The cowardice *and* the love are significant, only great love makes the cowardice moving, and not merely abject. Amaranta's vocation is to miss love, and painfully to cherish the knowledge of all she is missing, to maintain intact her raw, intentional regret:

When she listened to the waltzes of Pietro Crespi she felt the same desire to weep that she had had in adolescence, as if time and harsh lessons had meant nothing. The rolls of music that she herself had thrown into the trash . . . kept spinning and playing in her memory.
[241: 258]

This music is like the sobs of an infant which echo through a whole adult life in Proust's novel, and it is in this passage of *One Hundred Years of Solitude* that we read of the fragrant and worm-eaten guava grove, the terrible burden of ungiven love which Amaranta is dragging toward death. She has the reverse of Rebeca's 'impatient heart': a heart which in the end possesses only its own desperate patience.

The story of Remedios the Beauty, who is named after Aureliano's dead wife, is more 'like a bolero' than anything in the novel, including the trickle of the dead man's blood, yet it seems curiously separate as an anecdote, almost an interpolated tale. There is a connection to all the dark love songs though, and it is worth pursuing, since it allows us to place Amaranta's vocation on a more general map of desire.

Remedios is a girl of astonishing beauty and unearthly innocence, who drives men to their doom but doesn't know what all the fuss is about. The men simply die of their passion, or commit suicide; a foreigner who watches her bathing falls from a roof to his death; a banana-worker who touches her in a crowd boasts of his prowess and is killed by a horse. She is said to possess 'powers of death', and even the scent of her skin is called 'mortal' [206: 220–221]. Yet 'until her last moment on earth' she is unaware that she is a 'daily disaster', 'un desastre cotidiano', that her 'destiny' is that of the 'perturbing female' [203: 217]. 'Perhaps', the narrator speculates with a characteristic, unsettling injection of freedom into destiny, 'a feeling as primitive and as simple as that of love' would have been enough to dispel her awful powers, 'but that was the only thing that did not occur to anyone' [207: 221]. Love, that is, as distinct from ogling, desiring, despairing, slavering and generally being knocked over by beauty. The mention of Remedios' 'last moment on earth' is a quiet joke in the line of sly prophecies, since it does not mean, as it seems to, the day she dies, but literally her last moment *on earth*, before she ascends to heaven, one afternoon when she is helping to fold sheets. García Márquez' touch of comic precision in the midst of miracle is to have her take the sheets with her as she goes, lifting off into the upper air 'where not even the highest-flying birds of memory could reach her' [208: 223]

By sending Remedios beyond memory García Márquez no doubt means to suggest she can only be imagined, like so much else in this book. The imagined, as we have seen, need not be the merely fanciful. It may be just what we need to know. The logic of the bolero here comes very close to the logic of a fairy tale, or indeed that of Dostoyevsky's *Idiot*, another universe where innocence is both appealing and lethal. The story of Remedios concerns the perfect simplicity of beauty, and the damage it can do, if we cannot match its simplicity. It is a story therefore which half-validates Amaranta's fear, since it confirms the world of desire as a world of death, a place of magical, murderous perils; and half-condemns it, since death and danger may occur only as the result of love's absence – of a forgetting or failure of love. Remedios herself is too simple (or too lucid) to fall in love; her world is not simple enough to think of love as a pacifying possibility. Between these two abstentions lie all the frights and refusals of the novel; and either way, as a contemporary critical song might have it, love is just a theory, the redemption which practice lacks.

Trails of incest

I don't want to say too much about incest in *One Hundred Years of Solitude*, because literary incest is too easily allegorized, and critics have already had a field day, but it is a plight of the *family*, and I need to note García Márquez' insistent allusions to it.

The trickle of blood from José Arcadio's corpse finds its way through the village to his mother. Is this an instance of traditional filial loyalty reaching beyond death or a belated, bolero-flavoured Oedipal wish? When the same José Arcadio, as a boy, is drawn to Pilar Ternera, he wants to 'be with her all the time', wants her to 'be his mother' [29: 33]. Critics like Joset and Palencia-Roth pounce on the intimation of incest here, but surely the suggestion is more delicate than that. This is inexperience bowled over by the first stirrings of sexual desire. The boy is not Oedipus, he just thinks all femininity is the domain of the mother, and can't think of another image for what he wants. However, when he finds his way to Pilar in the dark, he tries to remember her face, and remembers his mother's instead, 'confusedly aware that he was doing something that for a very long time he had wanted to do but that he had imagined could really never be done' [31: 34–35]. The language is now carefully ambiguous. The boy's ordinary fascination and dread of sexual initiation are no doubt primary, but the shadow of incest certainly hovers here too. More luridly, there is perhaps a hint that sex *is* incest, that incest is what we might ultimately discover behind the many masks and incarnations that sexuality adopts.

Palencia-Roth thinks there is 'subconscious incest' in the novel when a woman behaves maternally to her lover, and 'metaphorical incest' when José Arcadio sleeps with and then

marries Rebeca, whom he calls his sister. There is something
in the second case, and it is interesting that the notion of incest should so circle round José Arcadio, and that he should
be brought to light. This darkness would include inexplicable
incest is not so much a temptation or a danger in *One Hundred Years of Solitude* as a figure for a sort of darkness in the
world of the novel, a gesture toward everything which can't
be brought to light. This darkness could include inexplicable
events and inscrutable motivations: the whole realm of the
unsayable. Still, the instance of José Arcadio and Rebeca,
who know they are *not* brother and sister, does need con-
trasting with its logical opposite, that of Arcadio's wanting to
sleep with his mother although he is not aware that that is
what she is. If he had managed it, it would have been incest,
no doubt about it, but his desire itself seems innocent, merely
uninformed. Unless we want to argue (but on what basis,
other than critical zeal?) that his desire somehow knows the
hidden story of his parentage.

There is metaphorical incest, then, which may feel real
enough; and there is real incest averted. Aunts and nephews
long for each other, the aunt in two cases being Amaranta;
and in the last case of all, that of Aureliano Babilonia and
Amaranta Úrsula, they become lovers. Cousins marry, and
are afraid of producing a race of iguanas. There is a prece-
dent. An aunt of Úrsula's married an uncle of José Arcadio
Buendía's, and they had a child with a pig's tale, source of
all the family mythology on the subject. The men tend not to
worry so much about the problem, or at least talk as if they
didn't. 'I don't care if I have piglets', José Arcadio Buendía
says, 'as long as they can talk' [25: 28]. Aureliano José,
beseeching Amaranta to sleep with him, is told that one needs
a papal dispensation to marry one's aunt. 'And not only
that', Amaranta says. 'Any children will be born with a pig's
tail.' Aureliano José is undeterred, continues to plead: 'I
don't care if they're born armadillos . . .' [135–136: 145]. In
a splendid joke in just this context, Aureliano José asks a
soldier whether a man can marry his aunt. 'Not only can he
do that', the soldier replies, 'but we are fighting this war

against the priests so that a person can marry his own mother'
[135: 145]. A new definition of anti-clericalism.

García Márquez himself has said that what interested him
above all in the novel was 'to tell the story of a family obsessed by incest'. But the obsession is both intermittent and
burlesqued, and therefore hard to treat as a stable theme. It
is a threat, certainly, the name of a terror, but it doesn't
always terrify. It is obviously the sexual form of solitude, a
failure to imagine the way out of the family, to make contact
with the world. But there are also times when it feels less
literary, less tautological. Then it doesn't terrify but troubles,
as if it had to stand for a guilt which has other names, or can't
be named. Or for a region where guilt lives but ought not to
live.

When told by Pietro Crespi that Rebeca is his sister, José
Arcadio says not that she isn't but that he doesn't care. Informed that his act (in marrying her) is against nature and
against the law, he says he shits twice on nature, and doesn't
even mention the law [88: 95]. There is no incest here, but
there is an indifference to it which may amount to a form of
transgression. Aureliano Babilonia and Amaranta Úrsula are
afraid they may have the same father − Aureliano learns the
truth from Melquíades' manuscripts only as the town and the
novel end − but take refuge in a fable about his being a
foundling. Their not knowing may go even further than José
Arcadio's not caring, and of course they are nephew and
aunt. Desire defies human laws and what we call nature, but
it *is* nature, a lurch of the unruly reality beneath the labels.
There is an innocence of desire, and the writer's flirting with
incest may be a way of insisting on the extremity of the innocence. It is significant, as Suzanne Jill Levine notes, that
the most erotic scenes in the book are those closest to incest,
metaphorical or literal, and I guess the celebration of brothels
as pastoral havens from all kinds of moral storm belongs to
the same movement of thought. You take a forbidden reality
and, instead of defending it, you purify it. You purify it, but
you can't protect it, and I think we should see all the distress
and damage which surround the final innocence of Aureliano

Babilonia and Amaranta Úrsula as signs not only of the extremity of their innocence but of its fragility and unlikeliness too. There is no punishment of incest: incest in the novel is innocence dogged by guilt, not guilt getting its comeuppance. What does get its terrible comeuppance is not guilt but happiness.

The threat of happiness

The cards appear to be stacked against the Buendías in love – or at least against any love which might lead them out of their solitude. Disease and bad luck will ruin romance, even if fear and pride don't, and the sudden death of little Remedios, in particular, would seem savagely gratuitous, like the death of Cordelia in *King Lear*, if it didn't seem so firmly designed to keep Colonel Aureliano Buendía away from happiness – just in case his solitary character shouldn't entirely do the trick. Meme Buendía, as we have seen, was sociable and in love, had none of the family's supposed vocation for solitude, until an absurd accident masquerading as fate crippled her lover and sent her to a convent. This is a proof either that fate gets you in the end, or that when you are got you call it fate.

The implication then is not of a generalized, Proustian impossibility of love but of something stranger, more restrictive. Aureliano Segundo doesn't get on with his wife Fernanda but finds both passion and calm with Petra Cotes, and the novel is full of warm-hearted, sexually welcoming women – Petra, Pilar Ternera, Santa Sofía de la Piedad, the friendly inhabitants of both real and imaginary brothels – who plainly serve to demystify the dark bolero. They show that love *can* be easy and doom-free, and they are a crucial axis, the relaxed norm against which nightmares are measured. What is significant is that none of them is a Buendía. They are the antithesis of the strict and industrious Úrsula; of the frightened Amaranta; of the unaroused Remedios the Beauty; of the frigid Fernanda, who becomes a Buendía by marriage and also by acceding to what might be called their legacy of solitude.

The family doom thus seems entirely set. There are avoidable destinies in the novel, but this is not one of them. The effect finally is that of a magical rule, something like the prohibition of love in Thomas Mann's *Dr Faustus*. The rule is that races condemned to one hundred years of solitude not only don't have a second opportunity on earth [360: 383], they don't have a chance to love even in their first and only term. They *can't* love, except in isolated cases which highlight the general force of the rule. This sometimes reflects a fact of character and sometimes a sort of conspiracy of events. In other words the Buendías often can't bring themselves to love, but are also on occasion literally prevented from loving. Simply to say they are incapable of love is to deny the conspiracy against them, to miss the weird collusion between chance and their weakness – chance in novels, we remember, being nothing other than the careful simulation of the unplanned. There are all kinds of obstacles to love for the Buendías, and their variety illustrates the complexity of the point.

The great interest of the stormy romance between Aureliano Babilonia and Amaranta Úrsula, the last couple in the book, is that it threatens to convert solitude into happiness, thereby confounding the whole dark conceptual framework of the fiction. They seem to have found the love that was lacking in the story of Remedios the Beauty, and indeed almost everywhere else, and of course if they have found this love, then the very notion of a magical rule or a family doom evaporates, turns retrospectively into a long but not unending chapter of reclusions and mischances.

We have heard of the 'paradise of shared solitude' [295: 313] which is Aureliano Segundo's and Petra's love, but the key words pile up with feverish intensity, and with new colours, in the last chapter of the novel. Macondo becomes lonely again, 'forgotten even by the birds', and Aureliano and Amaranta Úrsula are 'secluded by solitude and love and by the solitude of love' [349: 371]. They are 'the only happy beings, and the most happy on the face of the earth' [349: 372], a tautology which manages to sound delirious about their happiness. There is a slightly clumsy moralizing in the prose, a clawing back of these characters on to a path of recognizable virtue, when their love is said to settle down — they exchange salacity for solidarity [352: 375], crazy fornication for an affection based on loyalty [355: 378] — but the exhilaration of this last wild adventure remains. Aureliano and Amaranta Úrsula make love in the pool and the patio, break up the furniture and are said to do more damage than the encroaching red ants. They are close to becoming 'a single being', that ultimate creature of incest, and they are 'more and more integrated into the solitude of the house' [354: 376]. Their world is a 'paradise of poverty' [355: 378], a 'paradise of disasters' [350: 373]. There are ambiguities here, of course, and a hint that happy love has its price. The sad words retain their sadness, solitude *is* solitude even if it's bliss, and the world may crumble around you. But by the same token paradise *is* paradise even if it's a ruin, and the lovers cheerfully pay the price of isolation. Their child is said to be the only infant 'in a century' to be conceived in love [356: 378] — a commentary on and a challenge to the title of the novel. And then the horror strikes, a price of an entirely different kind is exacted. The child has a pig's tail, and Amaranta Úrsula dies soon after bearing him. The child itself, abandoned by Aureliano in his misery, is eaten by the ants.

García Márquez has repeatedly expressed his enthusiasm for Sophocles' *Oedipus Rex* ('the most important book in my life'), where a perfectly arbitrary prophecy is fulfilled down to the last letter. The arbitrariness is as important as the fulfilment. The child with the pig's tail looks at first sight like a completed oracle, like the late arrival of what should have happened a hundred years before, the prodigy which was to attend the marriage of the cousins José Arcadio Buendía and Úrsula Iguarán. But only the shape of this particular narrative turns this old superstition into a biological penance, a debt finally collected. 'They would have been happy', we learn of those first cousins, 'if Úrsula's mother had not terrified her with all manner of sinister predictions about their offspring' [25: 28]. 'Hubieron sido felices': the phrase perfectly balances the unanswerable question. They would have been happy, the whole destiny of the Buendías eluded, because superstitions come true only when you listen to them and believe in them? They would have been (ignorantly) happy because they would not have thought about the doom which nevertheless awaited their children? The pig's tail at the end violently endorses the second reading, of course, but it also asks us to think about the other one. It isn't a matter of rewriting the ending, only of seeing how *written* it is, the result of visible decisions taken. The rival story, the story of the escape from the prophecy, is not excluded, it is dangled before us and then brutally abolished, like Lucy Snowe's marriage at the end of Charlotte Brontë's *Villette*. And even the prophecy, thoroughly vindicated in the pig's tail, scarcely calls for Amaranta Úrsula's bleeding to death, and the devouring of the child.

The last lovers appear to break the magical rule of *One Hundred Years of Solitude*, and are spectacularly, terminally punished – are punished, I suggest, not for their incest but for being happy in love. I'm tempted to speak of reckless authorial cruelty here, but the narrative gesture is not quite that. Certainly the rule is saved only by the writer's eager insistence on it, but this represents what I take to be a scruple and a conflict. García Márquez can't make his last or any central characters happy, they are Buendías, emblems of a whole charming but imprisoned culture. Yet he really does seem to believe in the unearned, transgressive happiness that Aureliano Babilonia and Amaranta Úrsula achieve, and the haste and harshness with which he recruits and aggravates the old prophecy is a mark of the trouble they are causing. Their crime, I think, is their successful escape from history – the very history everyone else is disastrously forgetting. They almost redeem solitude, and one can see why a novelist, however drawn to them, would hesitate to let them wreck his plot and title and all his moral and political implications.

They really need a new novel, they are more than Melquíades or Gabriel bargained for. Perhaps García Márquez was thinking of this effect when he said that his earlier books finished on the last page, belonged to 'a kind of premeditated literature that offers too static and exclusive a vision of reality'.

Chapter 7

Aureliano's smile

'She cannot do without shooting, Gedali', I told the old man,
'because she is the Revolution.'   Isaac Babel

Colonel Aureliano Buendía is the most complex and haunting
character in *One Hundred Years of Solitude*, although not the
most forceful or the most necessary to life in Macondo. We
are in his mind in the first sentence of the book, and worrying
about his vanished political legacy on the last pages. He is
austere, distant, yet oddly appealing, and seems to provoke
in others an irresistible urge to simplify him — the others including many critics, many readers, García Márquez himself
and Aureliano's mother Úrsula. There is also at one point a
sort of drift in the character, an uncertainty in the narrator's
hold on him, which threatens to take him quite out of focus,
beyond simplification but also beyond understanding.

A daguerrotype of Aureliano as a child is described — he
is between Amaranta and Rebeca, wears a black velvet suit,
has 'the same languor and the same clairvoyant look that he
was to have years later as he faced the firing squad' [51: 56]
— but he permitted no photographs during his military days
or after. The Buendía children of a later generation are told
that a Tartar horseman in an encyclopaedia is Aureliano
because 'in spite of his strange outfit' he has 'a familiar (or
a family) air', 'un aire familiar' [280: 297]. And of course
this *is* a picture of Aureliano, of the kind this book
affords: his bony face and drooping moustache give him the
oriental appearance so common in Latin America, and his
spells of tyranny suggest some Asiatic scourge. But the gag
also insists that the only picture we have of him as an

91

adult is a picture of someone else, and from half the world away at that – a joking metaphor for our need of metaphor.

There are pictures of Aureliano outside the text, since he is the one character with a particularly marked historical source. Clearly all the characters have sources – how could they not? – and García Márquez has spoken of making up 'jigsaw puzzles of many different people and, naturally, bits of myself as well'. But Aureliano is an allusion as well as a character. He has the rank attained by García Márquez' own grandfather in the Liberal Army in Colombia's War of the Thousand Days, but he has the power, career and angular looks of General Rafael Uribe Uribe, leader of the Liberal forces in the same war. Uribe fought in various insurrections, all abortive, starting as early as 1876; was elected to the House of Representatives; waged the long war; signed the Peace of Neerlandia; was assassinated in 1914 – unlike Aureliano, who dies quietly at home on a day when the circus comes to town. The General was immensely popular, and as Stephen Minta says, 'perhaps the strangest aspect of Uribe Uribe's life and military career was the way in which he was able to preserve a glorious reputation unscathed through a wealth of defeats'. Of course it may be that failure is essential to such a reputation, that success would only wreck it, and that we can understand the historical Uribe through the fictional Aureliano; that Aureliano is a reading of Uribe as well as an allusion to him, an exploration of the legend. Lucila Inés Mena puts the matter very well:

Colonel Aureliano Buendía embodies the whole of Liberal history in the period. He is a synthesis of the rebellion, with its leaders, its ideals and its failures. On the other hand, the colonel is the war . . .

He is the war. He is at first solitary decency dragged into war. He has very little grasp of the issues involved but a strong instinct for justice, and the political situation is evoked around him with a casual lucidity, an apparent offhandedness which is itself a form of commentary. The customary dead-pan of the narrative tone here edges toward brilliant caricature.

Aureliano receives 'schematic lessons' in current affairs from his father-in-law, the Conservative *corregidor*. The Liberals, Don Apolinar says, are

freemasons, bad people, wanting to hang priests, to institute civil marriage and divorce, to recognize the rights of illegitimate children as equal to those of legitimate ones, and to cut the country up into a federal system that would take power away from the supreme authority. The Conservatives, on the other hand, who had received their power directly from God, proposed the establishment of public order and family morality. They were the defenders of the faith of Christ, of the principle of authority, and were not prepared to permit the country to be broken down into autonomous entities.

[90: 97]

Aureliano has an illegitimate son and leans to the Liberals for that reason. But he would lean to them anyway, and his first insight into the electoral process confirms his preference. The election has been quite proper and well-conducted, as far as the actual voting is concerned. Don Apolinar has the votes counted. They are very close, so he removes most of the Liberal ballots and makes up the numbers with Conservative ballots. 'The Liberals will go to war', Aureliano says, amazed, but Don Apolinar says not: that is why a few Liberal ballots were left in the box. The next exchange is worthy of Stendhal on French electioneering:

Aureliano understood the disadvantages of being in the opposition. 'If I were a Liberal', he said, 'I'd go to war because of those ballots.' His father-in-law looked at him over his glasses.
    'Oh, Aurelito', he said, 'if you were a Liberal, even though you're my son-in-law, you wouldn't have seen the switching of the ballots.'   [91: 98]

Don Apolinar's 'Ay' in 'Ay, Aurelito' is really untranslatable: much wisdom and history and sadness in such *ays*.

But what takes Aureliano to war is not Conservative vote-fixing but government-supported violence. The war has started, the military have taken over from Don Apolinar, who retains only an ornamental jurisdiction in Macondo, and four soldiers brutally kill a woman who has been bitten by a rabid dog. Aureliano and his friends, armed with kitchen knives and sharpened bits of iron, capture the garrison, and shoot the captain and the four offending soldiers. Aureliano's career has begun.

We should pause to note the movie logic here. Aureliano doesn't understand 'how people arrived at the extreme of waging war over things that could not be touched with the hand' [91: 97]. He is like Gary Cooper or Humphrey Bogart, unmoved by abstractions but provoked by cruelty, by the sight of victimization. This is the way that American isolation, another long solitude, ends in film after film. We don't need to think about the movies themselves in any detail, only to see that Aureliano is behaving here like a legend, like a simplification. He *is* moved by abstractions when they are close enough, as the matter of the vote shows, and I don't mean to underestimate decency as a political motive, far from it. I do want to suggest that the purity of Aureliano's response allows an effect that William Empson would call pastoral: we don't disbelieve the simplification, but we do know the world is more complex, indeed the simplification itself seems to glance at what it leaves out.

In fact Aureliano's position is not a political one at all, but a moral response to a political world, and many ambiguities in the novel revolve around our feelings about this response. Is it haughty and unrealistic, for example, or a rare instance of honesty and dignity? The same questions can be asked, not coincidentally and with unusual frequency, about many gestures, past and present, in Latin American politics. At times Aureliano seems blinkered or self-deluding, his strategy a form of solitude. At others he seems to be taking the only untainted stance there is, and there are moments when his very failure seems to assure his integrity, to be all that decency could ever expect.

In the midst of the civil wars he is busy losing, Aureliano appears to turn into a sort of Shakespearean tyrant, wishing a rival dead, and then executing the eager lieutenant who anticipates his wish. He has a chalk circle drawn around him wherever he goes, and from its centre he decides 'the destiny

of the world' [148: 159]. He is 'lost in the solitude of his immense power' [149: 160], and says things like 'The best
friend a person has is one who has just died' [149: 161]. He
comes close to executing his old comrade Gerineldo Márquez
because they disagree about the terms of a peace, and his
mother swears to kill him if he carries out the sentence, saying
'It's exactly what I would have done if you'd been born with
a pig's tail' [152: 163]. He is a monster, a 'mythical warrior'
[153: 165] who seems to be everywhere and whom no one can
kill. He is told that his heart is 'rotting alive' [148: 159], and
he himself later thinks his affections have 'rotted' [155: 167].
He contracts an 'inner coldness' [149: 160] which is never to
leave him, and which is a grim, displaced reflection of the ice
that delighted him as a child.

The 'destiny of the world' and the 'immense power' are
either delusions on Aureliano's part or verbal flourishes on
García Márquez'. Aureliano has the power of life and death
that any bandit or gangster has, but he really would need to
win a battle or two to have the tremendous power this rhetoric
suggests. We seem to be reading a trial run for the dictator-
novel García Márquez was later to write as *Autumn of the
Patriarch*, with its mingled horror and fascination for the
loneliness and folly of men who actually do decide vast
destinies. But then here, in *One Hundred Years of Solitude*,
García Márquez lets go of Aureliano the tyrant almost as
soon as he has picked him up. 'The intoxication of power
began to fall apart in gusts of uneasiness ['ráfagas de
desazón' literally gusts of insipidity, flavourlessness, barren-
ness, or discomfort] . . . He felt scattered . . . and more
solitary than ever' [149: 160–161]. This is not the solitude of
power, it is the solitude that neither power nor anything else
can change, and another phrase takes us even closer to the
problem. 'Only he knew', we are told of Aureliano, 'that his
confused heart was condemned to uncertainty for ever': 'su
aturdido corazón,' his confused or bewildered heart [148:
159]. The coldness and the spoiling of the affections are a
way of dealing with bewilderment; of freezing it.

However, if Aureliano is not an imperial tyrant, he is for

a time a harsh military commander, and an image of how loneliness can look like heartlessness. He has not become like his enemies through fighting them, as an intelligent opponent suggests [144: 154], because he is and remains the opposite of the ambitious and time-serving military. He is unbendingly honest and principled, willing to have this same opponent executed, although he likes and admires him, because 'it's the Revolution' that is doing the shooting, and the other man would have done the same in his place [143: 153]. But there is certainly a stoppage of feelings in Aureliano, and some self-deception: we are reading a fable about the corruption of incorruption. When Aureliano looks at José Raquel, the man he is about to have killed, he sees him 'with his heart':

He was startled to see how much he had aged, how his hands shook, and the rather routine air of acceptance ['la conformidad un poco rutinaria'] with which he awaited death, and then he felt a profound contempt for himself which he took for the beginnings of pity.   [143–144: 154]

This is an extraordinary insight, but kept just beyond the reach of the character. Aureliano despises the depth of his own mistake. A man who didn't recognize abstractions is about to have an abstraction kill a man he would rather keep alive. But even now Aureliano himself doesn't understand his own response. He feels the self-contempt but thinks it is pity. His heart is in worse shape than he thinks.

As I have suggested, García Márquez loses sight of Aureliano at times, or rather wants him for too many jobs. But this slippage of interest (unintended, I take it) does mirror Aureliano's own central uncertainty. Among the five volumes of verse Aureliano has written is a poem about a man who went out into the rain and got lost, 'el poema del hombre que se había extraviado en la lluvia' [115: 123]. A similiar misfortune occurs in 'Isabel watching the rain in Macondo', except that the man gets lost in time, 'se extravío en el tiempo'. Aureliano − the word *extraviado* is used of him too [149: 160] − is a man who gets lost in time and the war, one of history's strays. And in this rainy light his recurring self-contempt must be less a justified verdict than an intense and tangled response to his own bewilderment, the raging of his confused heart. Guilt is at least better than helplessness; a tormenting alternative to freezing the feelings. Power for Aureliano is not the world of politics he despises or even the licence to order life and death, it is everything he feels called upon to do single-handed, his lonely mission against the world's wrongs: an expression of his altruism but also of his arrogance.

Aureliano tries, with some success, not to permit himself emotions. When his little bride Remedios dies his reaction is not the 'commotion he feared' but only a 'dull feeling of rage that gradually dissolved into a solitary and passive frustration, similar to the one he had felt during the time when he had resigned himself to celibacy' [90: 97]. 'We see', Jacques Joset comments in his edition, 'that Aureliano's feeling for Remedios was not exactly love.' Is this what we see? Surely we see a man who is chronically afraid of feeling, romantically risks it, and retreats into cold fury when calamity occurs. Aureliano's response is the same when sixteen of his sons are massacred, a 'dull anger', 'una cólera sorda', which puts a frightening glint back into his eyes – of the kind that at other times made chairs move just because he looked at them [212: 226–227].

As had happened with the death of his wife, as had happened to him so many times during the war with the deaths of his best friends, he did not have a feeling of sorrow but a blind and directionless rage, an extenuating impotence.   [211: 226]

This looks less like an inability to love than an inability to mourn, abetted perhaps by a strangled regret, the belated, self-protecting thought that it would have been better to have felt nothing at all.

The dryness of Aureliano's heart, the coldness of his entrails which is said to be a source of vitality [141: 151], are both a mask and a desolate achievement – since the mask can no longer be lifted or distinguished from the face. Aureliano's defence against nostalgia, for example, is horribly secure. The past holds out 'insidious traps' for him, shows him that his mother at least understands his unhappiness. He gazes at her face, her leathery skin, decayed teeth, faded hair, her dazed look; sees the scars and scratches that half a century of daily life has left on her; but cannot even feel pity. At this moment, we are told, Remedios is only the blurred image of someone who might have been his daughter, and his countless mistresses in the wars have left no trace in his feelings [154–155: 166–167]. He has a gruesome memory which confirms rather than contradicts his immunity to nostalgia. One eleventh of October he woke in bed with a woman who was dead. He remembers the date because she had asked him about it an hour before, but he didn't know her name or see her face, because she came to him in the darkness, as so many women did. And he doesn't remember that she was drowning in tears, and swore to love him till she died. Only the text, and Melquíades, remember for him, and let us see the pathos of the woman's too quickly kept promise [231: 247].

Aureliano does have moments of what he would call weakness. 'Caught at last in one of nostalgia's traps', he confusedly remembers the nameless girl who in a later García Márquez story was to be called Eréndira. Perhaps if he had married her he would have been 'a man without war and without glory, a nameless artisan, a happy animal' [157: 168–169]. Perhaps. The scenario is improbable, *only* nostalgic, but revealing all the same. Eréndira is a girl who accidentally caused a fire in her grandmother's house, and is now brutally subject to prostitution until she has paid off the value of the property. She has already slept with seventy-three men the night the young Aureliano meets her, and reckons she has about ten years to go, at seventy men a night, before her debt is cancelled. Aureliano feels 'an irresistible need to love her and protect her' [53: 58], but when he looks for her again she and her grandmother have moved on.

The victim to be protected is repeated in Remedios, the child-bride. There is fear and solitude in such a choice, of course; perhaps an incapacity for a love which would not flatter pride, would not look like a favour. But there is generosity too, the same spirit we have seen in Aureliano's political impulses, and something not felt at all by Eréndira's other

seventy clients a night, or by most suitors of grown-up girls
with nice dowries. Aureliano finds Remedios, we are told, not
in any of the material places where he might seek her, but
'only in the image that saturated his private and terrible
solitude' [64: 69]. This is a Proustian passion, all in the
obsessed mind, but the girl and her emerald eyes do exist, and
Aureliano does marry her. The saturated solitude ends, and
part of our distress at Remedios' sudden death must be
distress *for* Aureliano, for the road which can now only lead
back to loneliness.

Úrsula's theory about her son is harsher than this, more
deeply rooted in magic and in her own guilt. Aureliano cried
inside her before he was born, and she was sure this was the
first indication that the child would have the dreaded pig's
tail. She 'begged God to let the child die in her womb' [218:
233]. Later she sees, with what is called 'the lucidity of
decrepitude', that a baby's crying before birth is 'an une-
quivocal sign of the inability to love'. She also sees that

Colonel Aureliano Buendía had not lost his love for the family
because he had been hardened by the war, as she had thought before,
but that he had never loved anyone, not even his wife Remedios or
the countless one-night women who had passed through his life, and
much less his sons . . . He had not fought so many wars out of
idealism, as everyone had thought, nor had he given up an imminent
victory because of weariness, as everyone had thought, but had won
and lost for one and the same reason, pure and sinful pride.
[218: 233]

This is a comprehensive theory, not lightly to be dismissed.
There is nothing in the text to distance the author from it, and
plenty outside the text to suggest that he agrees. And the
theory must in large part be right. Aureliano himself suspects
his own idealism, and diagnoses pride:

One night he asked Colonel Gerineldo Márquez:
'Tell me something, old friend: why are you fighting?'
'What other reason could there be, old friend?' Colonel Gerineldo
Márquez answered. 'For the great Liberal Party.'
'You're lucky you know', he answered. 'As far as I'm concerned,
I've only just realized that I'm fighting out of pride.'

'That's bad,' Colonel Gerineldo Márquez said.

Colonel Aureliano Buendía was amused at his alarm. 'Naturally,' he said. 'But in any case, it's better than not knowing why you're fighting. He looked him in the eyes and added with a smile:

'Or fighting, like you, for something that doesn't have any meaning for anyone.'   [124: 133]

What Úrsula can't see — the lucidity of decrepitude must be some way from omniscience — and what García Márquez has forgotten is Aureliano's irony, his amusement at Gerineldo's alarm, his smile as he puts his old friend on the spot. Aureliano's diagnosis of pride is correct but simplified, far from the whole story: another version of pastoral.

His smile is frequently mentioned in the text, and quite often perceptible even without a mention — implicit in the wit of what he says. It is a smile which in no way denies pain or disillusionment or solitude, and is full of sadness. But I can't find any cynicism in it, only a bitter, balanced awareness of the grounds for despair and amusement. A man reads out a set of peace proposals which imply the abandonment of every principle the Liberals have stood for, to which Aureliano says *smiling*, 'You mean we're just fighting for power?' 'These are tactical reforms', one of the delegates says, and we don't need to be told that Aureliano's smile remains or what it means [150–151: 162].

One day Aureliano finds his mother weeping in the courtyard of their house, in the company of his father's ghost, which he has never seen and never will see:

'What does he say?' he asked.

'He's very sad,' Úrsula answered, 'because he thinks you are going to die.'

'Tell him,' the colonel smiled, 'that a person doesn't die when he should but when he can.'   [212: 227]

It must be hardness of heart, and his attempted refusal of the past, which prevent Aureliano from seeing his father's ghost, but there is a marvellously underplayed wisdom in his smiling epigram. At this moment he almost has the knowledge of Melquíades. He had premonitions as a child, knew when someone was coming, or when a pot was about to fall off a table. He can see the present and the immediate future, he reads minds, sees through his own and other people's illusions. He can picture, we are told, both sides of his thought [124: 133]. He can't see the splintered, retarded time in Melquíades' room, the magical release from dust and decay, but when Melquíades finally vanishes and the room succumbs to change, it is eerily said to be the room Aureliano had *foreseen* [312: 331]. Even his blindness is a form of sight: the problem is the misery of what he perceives, the wintry triumph of his lucidity. He is a writer, or has been, but is in this sense the exact opposite of our invisible novelist, who can't do without the past, who needs to see ghosts, and to enlist the power of fiction to fight fictions. This is what Aureliano's smile seems to say: that truth is scarce and bleak and not enough, but that knowledge of helplessness is still a form of knowledge.

Aureliano's continuing life in the novel enacts precisely this insight. He does not become a ghost, like his father, like Melquíades, inventors both of them, men of the imagination. He becomes a disputed memory, a lost integrity, a historical question. He is the truth no one believes, and his only visible legacy is a street name. 'Ah', Aureliano Babilonia says to a priest, 'then you don't believe it either':

'Believe what?'
'That Colonel Aureliano Buendía fought thirty-two civil wars and lost them all,' Aureliano answered. 'That the army hemmed in and machine-gunned three thousand workers and that their bodies were carried off on a train with two hundred coaches to be thrown into the sea.'
The priest measured him with a pitying look.
'Oh, my son,' he sighed. 'It would be enough for me to be sure that you and I exist at this moment.'   [354: 376]

The complicated twist here is that Colonel Aureliano Buendía is a model for both types of thought: for the stubborn resistance to official untruth, and for the habit of solitude which makes even one's own existence doubtful.

'Many years later, as he faced the firing squad, Colonel Aureliano Buendía was to remember that distant afternoon when his father took him to discover ice.' Years later still, facing only an apparently interminable old age, he remembers the ice again, the bright miracle which for him has become only a melancholy metaphor. The memory is triggered by the sound of a brass band and the happy cries of children. A circus has come to town, as if to say goodbye to Aureliano on behalf of all the colour and profusion of the life he has so austerely refused. He dies losing track of a thought:

He saw a woman dressed in gold sitting on the back of an elephant. He saw a sad dromedary. He saw a bear dressed like a Dutch girl keeping time to the music with a soup spoon and a pan. He saw the clowns doing cartwheels at the end of the parade and once more he saw the face of his miserable solitude when everything had passed by and there was nothing but the bright expanse of the street and the air full of flying ants with a few onlookers peering into the precipice of uncertainty. Then he went to the chestnut tree, thinking about the circus, and while he urinated he tried to keep on thinking about the circus, but he could no longer find the memory. He pulled his head in between his shoulders like a baby chick and remained motionless with his forehead against the trunk of the chestnut tree. The family didn't find out until the next day . . .   [233–234: 250]

He couldn't find the memory, 'ya no encontró el recuerdo.' He can't remember, isn't remembered. He is not the most necessary character in the book, but he is the most missed, the one we most need to understand. He is the first human being to be born in Macondo, and his humanity, however tenuous and chilled, is important. He is the novel's dark conscience. No wonder García Márquez was reluctant to have him die, and went upstairs trembling, he says, when he had written the words I have just quoted. His wife Mercedes knew at once what had happened. 'The colonel's dead', she said, and García Márquez himself lay on his bed and cried for two hours. This is not a sentimental story, and there is no contradiction between those tears and Aureliano's smile.

Chapter 8

The liberation of Macondo

It seems probable that if we were never bewildered there would never be a story to tell about us.　　　Henry James

I insisted at the beginning of this book on the Latin American context of *One Hundred Years of Solitude*, its engagement with a particular mingling of despair and possibility. And indeed I think it likely that the immense popularity of the book in its original language – it is said to have sold more copies than any book in Spanish since *Don Quixote* – has a great deal to do with the image of themselves it offered to Latin Americans: not so much a portrait of solitude as a portrait of the style and grace with which solitude has been and is borne. For the first time, perhaps, Latin Americans read a book that talked the way they talked (or wished they talked) when they were at their wittiest, most stubborn and most stoic. They didn't miss Aureliano's smile.

It would be, and has been, easy to sentimentalize this smile, and by implication to over-romanticize solitude, as long as one is not reading too carefully. There is a lot of anger in the book, as I have tried to show. It is a discreet anger, not at all noisy; but pretty powerful all the same. The story of the novel is the story of life inside the cage of an all-too enchanting myth.

But if we move our perspective a little, think of *One Hundred Years of Solitude* as read in translation, in any one of twenty-seven languages, or indeed read in Spanish in North America, say, or in Spain, the picture lightens considerably. The word *solitude* still echoes through the text, of course, but saddens it less; and readers are chiefly exhilarated and amazed. They are not looking into a stylish mirror, they are watching an astonishing tropical carnival of narrative, what a Spanish critic has called a 'phenomenal fiesta'. The same critic says the novel is a 'hymn to individual liberty'. I don't see how he can get *this* reading out of it, but the reversal of direction is very clear. There is little gloom or anger in these responses, and they are not simply false or misinformed. They are genuine responses to other, less historical, less contextual aspects of the work. García Márquez himself said he had 'an incredibly good time' writing the book, and kept laughing out loud as he went. There *is* a liberation here, and it is this liberation which makes the novel an international landmark as well as a native one.

The writers of the 'Boom', as I have suggested, freed themselves from an earnest, wrong-headed realism; but they also, and García Márquez principally among them, since he is by far the best-known in the world at large, freed other writers and their readers from other bondages. The bondages must be many, can scarcely be the same in England and America, or in Iran and Bulgaria, so guessing at their nature is particularly risky. It looks at first sight as if the bondage might be rationality, and what is welcomed is a domain of miracle and wonder, a fine refreshment for jaded epistemologies. There is a piece of truth in this, but only a piece.

In his novel *Flaubert's Parrot*, 1984, Julian Barnes beautifully lampoons this vogue:

A quota system is to be introduced on fiction set in South America. The intention is to curb the spread of package-tour baroque and heavy irony. Ah, the propinquity of cheap life and expensive principles, of religion and banditry, of surprising honour and random cruelty. Ah, the daiquiri bird which incubates its eggs on the wing; ah, the fredonna tree whose roots grow at the tips of its branches, and whose fibres assist the hunchback to impregnate by telepathy the haughty wife of the hacienda owner; ah, the opera house now overgrown by jungle . . . Novels set in the Arctic and the Antarctic will receive a development grant.

There is a tourism of the imagination, and at certain times it sells books. But the liberation offered by *One Hundred Years*

of Solitude is more durable and more substantive. It concerns
not miracles or easy exoticism − there are no camels in the
Koran, as Borges reminds us − but fiction itself, the profusion of stories in daily life, and the recovery of some of these
stories for literature. The rather surprising enemy may be not
realism but modernism.

'Oh dear, yes', E. M. Forster said, 'the novel tells a story.'
Forster was not a modernist, or not otherwise a modernist,
but he shared the modernists' distaste for mere, low narrative. Joyce and Woolf felt, no doubt rightly, that Edwar-
dian fiction had been bullied into shallowness by the demand
for plot, and that the plotless zones of the individual consciousness were a rich new territory for writers. They didn't
abandon narrative, of course, but they delayed and distended
and marginalized it. Their characteristic unit of time was a
thought-filled day; a period in which nothing much 'happened'. Or more precisely in which the very notion of something
'happening' came into question. A cup of cocoa might be
more of an event than an act of adultery; and a memory far
more of an event than either. The critical metaphor for this
emphasis in writing was 'spatial form', a sort of demotion of
time, and Lévi-Strauss later invented something like spatial
form for his study of myth − a sign among others that struc-
turalism was a delayed modernism. It is significant that the
return of a critical interest in time and narrative, for which
Frank Kermode's *The Sense of an Ending*, 1967, may stand
as an eloquent and convenient marker, follows and accom-
panies the reintroduction of stories into high-brow fiction.
They had, of course, never left popular fiction, or its film,
radio and television avatars. By the end of the 1960s, nothing
indicated more clearly a faded aesthetic, an allegiance to
yesterday's avant-garde than a continued aversion to story,
oh dear, yes.

But the story which returned was not the no-nonsense stuff
that Forster and the others had been resisting. On the con-
trary, it was full of nonsense, nonsense was its business. 'Late
one October afternoon my grandmother Anna Bronski was
sitting in her skirts at the edge of a potato field.' This is

Oskar, the narrator of Günter Grass' *The Tin Drum*, 1959, evoking a crucial figure in his life – remembering and reshaping her. He goes on to relate his mother's conception in this field – his grandmother shelters a fleeing patriot under her ample skirts – although neither his mother nor his grandmother, it turns out, will admit to this version of events. It must have been later that night, they say, or later altogether; it was raining and too windy in the field. Has Oskar invented this maculate conception? Well, he has perfected it, since his mother and grandmother do agree that the hidden patriot 'had done his best' in spite of the weather. There is no disagreement about the act, only about its outcome. There is no way in which the matter could be settled, and what makes the difference between the two versions of the story is imaginative need: Oskar wants a legendary, all-protecting grandmother, and his mother would rather not have been conceived in a potato patch. Much of the world is made up of stories in just this sense, fictions which take facts as their opportunities; and it seems strange that literature could have let go of them for so long. Because we couldn't trust them entirely, did we decide not to trust them at all?

Grass doesn't narrate using Oskar's grandmother's method, if she had one, but then García Márquez only figuratively follows his own grandmother. What both writers do is draw on what we might call the world of the grandmothers, the rich realm of old and young wives' tales, of gossip, extravagance and ghosts. It is this recourse which has transformed fiction in many countries, and which enacts the liberation I evoked. Miracle and wonder after all, then? Not quite.

One Hundred Years of Solitude is a landmark, but in literature, if not in geography, landmarks tend to cluster and unwittingly conspire. García Márquez joins forces with Grass because he is another redeemer of story, and both of them look back to William Faulkner. Faulkner remains the grand high modernist, of course, dedicated to frozen time and whirling states of consciousness, to inextricably ravelled, unprogressive narratives – no one ever read Faulkner for the story, in Forster's sense. But dead writers also continue to develop. As T. S. Eliot said, we should 'not find it preposterous that the past should be altered by the present as much as the present is directed by the past'. Borges, mischievously pursuing the same thought, suggests that 'every writer *creates* his own precursors'. In this light Faulkner emerges as the unmistakable ancestor of Grass and García Márquez because he relies so thoroughly, as they do, on the peculiar truthfulness even of lying stories. Such stories may simply be the only way of getting at a lost or cancelled or stagnant past. Young Quentin Compson, for example, in *Absalom, Absalom!* 1936, tries to find a sense for the American South, that place 'peopled with garrulous outraged baffled ghosts', and finds it only in the criss-crossing of the narratives he listens to and tells, in their weird corroborations and contradictions. 'It's because she wants it told', Quentin thinks of Rosa Coldfield's story; and he and his Canadian friend at Harvard create a shadow world out of 'the rag-tag and bob-ends of old tales and talking'.

Fiction mirrors fiction here, but such fiction, although different from fact, is no longer starkly opposed to it. Literature finds out and frames the literary quality of much ordinary life, the stories we keep teasing into action. Jacques Derrida's famous 'il n'y a pas de hors-texte' means not that everything is a text but that textuality skulks everywhere, even in the most material of monuments. This is still an exaggeration (everywhere?), but an illuminating one, and it helps us to see how deconstruction, as a critical mode, can accompany a renewed interest in narrative. Critics, novelists and philosophers ask, in the journalists' phrase, 'What's the story?'

The implication is that we live in a landscape shaped by our belief − that is, among all the things, true and untrue, which we take to be the truth − and that stories are the texture of such a world. Stories thus offer a fund of 'experience' much wider and more welcoming to the imagination than the dogged first-hand stuff that hard-boiled and even soft-boiled writers used to feel they needed. 'She spoke of experience',

Elizabeth Hardwick says of a girl in *Sleepless Nights*, 1979, 'meaning only previous work.' Novelists have often meant much the same: only their previous marriages and divorces and other real-life adventures. Henry James and Emily Brontë would have been dazed by the poverty of such a conception of experience, and what recent writers have nobly done is to destroy the tyranny of this thin authenticity. There is nothing wrong with authenticity, of course, and many books can't be written without it. But there is plenty wrong with tyranny. Writers now seem to take their knowledge where they find it – in their lives, in their minds, in the memories of their grandmothers, and even, as the work of Thomas Pynchon shows, in the once forbidden libraries. Novelists no longer have to pretend they don't read.

This larger, more generous sense of experience is very clear in the work of García Márquez' most distinguished successors in English, Salman Rushdie and Graham Swift. I don't see any major successors in Latin America, and this may reflect on the different liberations involved. I think we are now in a position to see what the second, international bondage may have been in one of its principal forms: not rationality, and not even modernism, which was perhaps only a symptom, but a widespread and often unconsciously harboured materialist prejudice, a commitment to whatever is glum and prosaic and concrete, as if reality were found nowhere else, as if truth inhabited only these sad reaches. This prejudice holds that facts are solid and that what is not solid is not a fact; that things are more important than words, the world more important than the mind. There is no point in simply asserting the reverse prejudice, in suggesting that the mind is more important than the world, and the rest. But it shouldn't be too hard to see the grotesque simplification implied in either preference. People have been horribly hurt by intangible facts, and even by plain untruths; words have done more damage in quarrels than flying crockery. Racism, for instance, is both a delusion and a fact: based on nothing, acted on by thousands. I think too of Lionel Trilling's subtle remark about money, which he says is 'both real and not real,

like a spook'. Indeed Trilling offers the best description I
know of the particular prejudice I am tracking: 'Reality is
always material reality, hard, resistant, unformed, im-
penetrable, and unpleasant.' Trilling thinks of this prejudice
as an American affliction, calls it a 'chronic American belief',
but I am suggesting it occurs almost everywhere, is absent
only in cultures untouched by our busy pragmatism. In places
like Macondo.

Of course reality often *is* hard, resistant, unformed, im-
penetrable and unpleasant, but an experience enlarged by
stories respects this reality and others, allows the mind and
the world to have their differences but remain entangled.
There are *verbatim* echoes of García Márquez in Salman
Rushdie, but they are less important than the splendid sense
of creative borrowing, the feeling in *Midnight's Children*,
1981, and *Shame*, 1983, that there is a way to India and
Pakistan through Macondo, that tall truths require tall tales.
There is a way to England too by the same route, and tracing
Graham Swift's work back to Faulkner and Grass as well as
to García Márquez helps to confirm my argument about the
clustering of landmarks and their combined effect.
Waterland, 1983, reclaims a long and fantastic family history
in the way that the fenland of the novel has been reclaimed
from the sea, and insists rather more than Rushdie's work
does on the truth which legends and myths are devised to conceal. Stories are a way of explaining the world, but explanations are a way of hiding from pain and difficulty: 'And we
do want out story. Yes, we can't do without our story.' Even
so, here as in the writers I have just mentioned, stories provide plenty of clues to what they themselves have hidden;
provide the only clues. Swift is less exuberant than either
Rushdie or García Márquez, and there may be a lingering
touch of Forster's 'Oh dear, yes' in him, but he is an important figure in the recovery of narrative.

Returning areas of experience to us, stories also restore
tired technique, since these rejuvenated novels can afford to
sound like stories. John Barth works at this insight in
Chimera, 1972, but rather clumsily. A story may or may not

be simple, but it will always look simple, and it is García Márquez' understanding of this principle which secures for him the effect that I have called pastoral in Empson's sense, an irony which seems to be an innocence. In 1969 and 1970, when translations of *One Hundred Years of Solitude* into French, Italian and English appeared, much literature in the world was, as Jack Richardson said, 'idiosyncratic and consciously complex', faithful to modernism's stern sense of difficulty. The result of the appearance of García Márquez' masterful ease on such a scene was not only to make us wonder whether the emperor really needed all the clothes he was wearing, but to change, as major work always does, our whole idea of literary dress and its relation to the body. The ease of *One Hundred Years of Solitude* was real as well as apparent, but the book was a feat of patience, since García Márquez had been thinking about it for fifteen or sixteen years.

Meanwhile we had been waiting for ages for an artist to overturn T. S. Eliot's dictum that modern writing had to be difficult: 'Our civilisation comprehends great variety and complexity, and this variety and complexity, playing upon a refined sensibility, must produce various and complex results.' We knew this was wrong, a version of the mimetic fallacy, but all the simple writers we enlisted in our cause turned out to be lightweights who seemed to prove Eliot's point, and all the good writers we could think of *were* difficult. The answer, as García Márquez even more than Grass taught us, was to renounce visible difficulty, the theory of difficulty, in the way that a joke renounces or ruins visible seriousness. 'I am a writer through timidity', García Márquez has said. 'My real vocation is that of a conjuror, but I get confused when I try to do a trick. . .' This gag illustrates the method of renunciation. It is simple and perfectly straight. There are no hidden meanings. But the remark is amusingly haunted by *absent* meanings, by all that is casually not said about real vocations, about the actual obstacles to writing and conjuring. Modern writing doesn't have to be difficult, but it probably does have to know the temptation of difficulty, to glance at the variety and complexity of the world. Its simplicity may still be quite genuine, not a front or a sham but an achievement of style. These are delicate matters, and we can scarcely begin to talk about them until we understand the elusive relation between seriousness and mischief.

Guide to further reading

Editions

Spanish texts of *Cien años de soledad* are readily available. There are those of Editorial Sudamericana, Buenos Aires, 1967, and Austral, Madrid, 1982, both with many reprintings. Jacques Joset's annotated edition (Cátedra, Madrid, 1984) has largely sensible commentary and makes useful connections to the rest of García Márquez' work. Much of García Márquez' journalism has been collected, with a valuable introduction, in Jacques Gilard, ed., *Obra periodística*, Bruguera, Barcelona, 1981–1984. There is also the reporting of the stories of others in *Relato de un náufrago*, Tusquets, Barcelona, 1970, and *La aventura de Miguel Littín clandestino en Chile*, El País, Madrid, 1986, both recently translated into English. The rest of the fiction is most easily found as follows:

El coronel no tiene quien le escriba, Era, Mexico City, 1961; Sudamericana, Buenos Aires, 1968; Bruguera, Barcelona, 1981.

La mala hora, Era, Mexico City, 1966; Bruguera, Barcelona, 1980.

La hojarasca, Sudamericana, Buenos Aires, 1969; Bruguera, Barcelona, 1981.

El otoño del patriarca, Plaza & Janés, Barcelona, 1975; Sudamericana, Buenos Aires, 1975; Bruguera, Barcelona, 1982.

Todos los cuentos (1947–1972), Plaza & Janés, Barcelona, 1975.

Crónica de una muerte anunciada, La Oveja Negra, Bogotá,

1981; Diana, Mexico City, 1981; Bruguera, Barcelona, 1981.
El amor en los tiempos del cólera, La Oveja Negra, Bogotá, 1985; Diana, Mexico City, 1985; Sudamericana, Buenos Aires, 1985; Bruguera, Barcelona, 1985.
El general en su laberinto, La Oveja Negra, Bogotá, 1989; Mondadori, Madrid, 1989.

Translations

Gregory Rabassa's version of *Cien años de Soledad* (Harper & Row, New York, 1970; Jonathan Cape, London, 1970; Avon, New York, 1971; Penguin, Harmondsworth, 1972; Picador, London, 1978) has errors but reads remarkably well. The remaining fiction is available as follows:
No one Writes to the Colonel and Other Stories, tr. J. S. Bernstein, Harper & Row, New York, 1968; Jonathan Cape, London, 1971; Avon, New York, 1973; Penguin, Harmondsworth, 1974; Picador, London, 1979. Contains the short novel of the title, and the eight stories which make up the Spanish volume *Los funerales de la Mamá Grande*, also found in *Todos los cuentos*.
Leaf Storm and Other Stories, tr. G. Rabassa, Harper & Row, New York, 1972; Jonathan Cape, London, 1972; Picador, London, 1979. Contains the novel of the title, four stories from the Spanish volume *La increíble y triste historia de la cándida Eréndira*, and two earlier stories, 'Nabo' and 'Monologue of Isabel watching the rain in Macondo'. All the stories are in *Todos los cuentos*.
The Autumn of the Patriarch, tr. G. Rabassa, Harper & Row, New York, 1976; Jonathan Cape, London, 1977; Picador, London, 1978.
Innocent Eréndira and Other Stories, tr. G. Rabassa, Harper & Row, New York, 1978; Jonathan Cape, London, 1979; Picador, London, 1981. Contains the title story, two other stories from the Spanish volume of the same name, and nine of the ten early stories collected in the Spanish volume *Ojos de perro azul*. Again, all the stories appear in *Todos los cuentos*.

In Evil Hour, tr. G. Rabassa, Harper & Row, New York, 1979. Jonathan Cape, London, 1980; Picador, London, 1982.
Chronicle of a Death Foretold, tr. G. Rabassa, Harper & Row, New York, 1982; Jonathan Cape, London, 1982; Picador, London, 1983.
Love in the Time of Cholera, tr. Edith Grossman, Knopf, New York, 1988; Jonathan Cape, London, 1988.

Bibliography and interviews

M. E. Fau's *Annotated Bibliography* (Greenwood Press, Westport, Connecticut, 1980) covers 1947–1979. There is an extremely good collection of interviews with the writer in A, Rentería Mantilla, ed., *García Márquez habla de García Márquez*, Rentería Editores, Bogotá, 1979. A lively interview is available in English in Rita Guibert, *Seven Voices*, Knopf, New York, 1973; and an extended conversation with the writer constitutes Plinio Apuleyo Mendoza's *El olor de la guayaba*, Bruguera, Barcelona, 1982, tr. Ann Wright as *The Fragrance of Guava*, Verso, London, 1983.

Background

I found Robert H. Dix, *Colombia: The Political Dimensions of Change*, Yale University Press, New Haven and London, 1967, most useful for Colombian history. Hubert Herring, *A History of Latin America*, Knopf, New York, 1968, is a standard text on the sub-continent. Lucila Inés Mena, *La función de la historia rn 'Cien años de soledad,'* Plaza & Janés, Barcelona, 1979, is a dogged but not dull account of historical parallels and antecedents for the novel. Jean Franco, *An Introduction to Spanish-American Literature*, Cambridge University Press, 1969, D. P. Gallagher, *Modern Latin American Literature*, Oxford University Press, 1973, and Gordon Brotherston, *The Emergence of the Latin American Novel*, Cambridge University Press, 1977, are lucid surveys of the literature. Carlos Fuentes, *La nueva novela hispano-*

americana, Joaquín Mortiz, Mexico City, 1969, and José
Donoso, *Historia personal del 'Boom'*, Anagrama,
Barcelona, 1972 (tr. G. Kolovakos as *The Boom in Spanish
American Literature*, Columbia University Press, New York,
1977) are engaging reports from the middle of the fray.

Criticism

Critical work on García Márquez has now reached industrial
proportions, and I can mention here only those studies I
thought especially helpful.
In English, G. R. McMurray, *Gabriel García Márquez*,
Ungar, New York, 1977, and R. L. Williams *Gabriel García
Márquez*, Twayne, Boston, 1984, offer sound introductions;
and Stephen Minta, *Gabriel García Márquez: Writer of
Colombia*, Jonathan Cape, London, 1987, is particularly
good on the later work. *Review 70*, Center for Inter-
American Relations, 1971, has a special supplement on the
novel, and includes the review by Jack Richardson which
I quote from on p. 110. Bernard McGuirk and Richard
Cardwell, eds., *Gabriel García Márquez: New Readings*,
Cambridge University Press, 1987, has some challenging
essays and an excellent bibliography. Two articles of exceptional interest and lucidity are Graham Burns, 'García
Márquez and the idea of solitude', *The Critical Review*, No.
27, 1985; and A. M. Taylor, '*Cien años de soledad*: history
and the novel', *Latin American Perspectives*, 2, no. 3, 1975.
In Spanish, Josefina Ludmer, '*Cien años de soledad*': *una
interpretación*, Tiempo contemporáneo, Buenos Aires, 1972,
is austere and intelligent and structuralist; Victor Farías, *Los
manuscritos de Melquíades*, Klaus Dieter Vervuert,
Frankfurt, 1981, is abstract and intelligent and Marxist.
Mario Vargas Llosa, *García Márquez: historia de un deicidio*,
Barral, Barcelona, 1971, is painstaking and pioneering, a
handsome tribute from one novelist to another. Suzanne Jill
Levine, *El espejo hablado*, Monte Ávila, Caracas, 1975, is a
short and lively book dedicated solely to *One Hundred Years
of Solitude*. Ricardo Gullón, *García Márquez o el olvidado*

arte de contar, Taurus, Madrid, 1970, and Jacques Joset, *Gabriel García Márquez, coetáneo de la eternidad*, Rodopi, Amsterdam, 1984, are even shorter, but full of insights. Michael Palencia-Roth, *Gabriel García Márquez: la línea, el círculo y las metamorfosis de mito*, Gredos, Madrid, 1983, is as overloaded as its title suggests, but raises interesting questions. Oscar Collazos, *García Márquez: la soledad y la gloria*, Plaza & Janés, Barcelona, 1983, is sensible and informative about the writer's career. F. E. Porrata and F. Avendaño, eds., *Explicación de 'Cien Años de soledad'*, Editorial Texto, San José, Costa Rica, 1976, has nineteen essays by various hands, and a bibliography. P. G. Earle, ed., *García Márquez*, Taurus, Madrid, 1981, collects seventeen good essays, including a translation of the Todorov piece I quote from on p. 60, and an article based on a conversation with the writer's father. It is here that we discover the doubt about the year of Gabriel García Márquez' birth, so the end of this note, appropriately, can be the beginning of a question. It is not only in Macondo that the truth is hard to find.